Fantastic, Fun Reading Programs

Kathryn Totten

Alleyside Press.

Fort Atkinson, Wisconsin

Published by **Alleyside Press**, an imprint of Highsmith Press
Highsmith Press
W5527 Highway 106
P.O. Box 800
Fort Atkinson, Wisconsin 53538-0800
1-800-558-2110

© Kathryn Totten, 2001
Cover design: Heidi Green

The paper used in this publication meets the minimum requirements of American National Standard
for Information Science — Permanence of Paper for Printed Library Material. ANSI/NISO Z39.48-
1992.

Library of Congress Cataloging-in-Publication Data
  Totten, Kathryn, 1955-
    Fantastic, fun reading programs / Kathryn Totten.
      p. cm.
  Includes bibliographical references.
    ISBN 1-57950-060-9 (alk. paper)
    1. Children's libraries–Activity programs–United States. 2.
  Children–Books and reading–United States. 3. Reading
  promotion–United States. I. Title.
  Z718.2.U6 T67 2001
  028.5–dc21   00-012523
                                          CIP

Contents

Introduction

Children are curious, energetic, and intelligent people. Those who work with them are constantly challenged to keep plenty of interesting activities planned. Providing opportunities for exploring knowledge in many fields, for developing social skills, and for exposure to the arts is the work of the program planner.

These simple, practical program plans require a minimum of your time to implement. Each of the five reading themes include eight programs. Their length and depth can be adapted to fit the needs of the community, the expected number of participants, your budget, and your time. In some cases they require a hired artist, but for most of them that is optional.

Programs for children cover a broad range of interests, including fine arts, science, literature, performing arts, and social studies. The library programs in this book are easily adapted to other settings, such as the classroom, a community center, Scouts other youth clubs, or a day care center.

Reading programs are meant to make the library a fun gathering place, inviting children to explore reading for pleasure. This program book provides opportunities for setting reading goals and receiving an award upon successful completion.

There are a number of ways to measure achievement in a reading program. One way is to count the number of titles read. The child may select the length of book that corresponds to his age and reading level. When a certain number of titles are read, the child receives an award. A variation is to count pages or time spent reading. In this book, suggested reading goals are flexible to match the reading levels of children from preschool through elementary school. They include counting book titles and counting number of pages read. They also offer the child the option of listening to someone reading to them, or to a recorded book. In some cases the goals are guided reading, offering suggestions for the child to explore poetry, recipes, newspapers and a variety of book genres. The program planner must use judgement, and adapt the reading goals to fit the needs of children in the community for which the reading program is planned.

Reading programs have traditionally been offered at public libraries during the summer months off from school. Children who read consistently during the summer return to school with their reading skills at least maintained, and often advanced. However, reading programs may be offered at any time of year, since some school districts now hold classes year-round, with breaks at a number of intervals.

Volunteers are very important for successful programs. They can assist with preparation for the event, help with managing the crowd, assist the children with crafts or games, and be available for last-minute needs. Young adults and parents are great candidates. Discuss with them well before the program exactly what you need them to do, and get a firm commitment from them.

Let *Fantastic, Fun Reading Programs* provide lasting inspiration for you and the children and families you serve!

1 Scrumptious Reading

The Scrumptious Reading theme is a delicious blend of stories, art, and fun. To tailor the programs to your audience, you may want to base them on ethnic foods popular in your community. There are many books for children with food themes, so it should be possible for you to display some all through your program. While playing with food is generally discouraged at the dinner table, as the Etiquette Tea will show, there are no rules that forbid creating art and games from edible items—such as pasta. A Milk Money service project that corresponds can help to give the children a sense of belonging and contributing to their community.

To encourage reading, a menu could be printed from which the children select their reading goal according to their age and reading level. A sample menu is included on p. 8, but again, tailor it to your participants' interests and culture.

Awards can be solicited from area restaurants, and could include chopsticks, food coupons, or food-shaped note pads. A pizza party could be given at the end of the theme for all children who reach their reading goal.

Scrumptious Reading Menu

Select your reading goal from the following choices.

Entrees

Pigs in a Blanket: Read three picture books or one chapter book about pigs while having a picnic. Your picnic may be indoors or outdoors.

Vegetable Soup: Read a poem, a story and a recipe. The poem and story may be about vegetables or food, if you like. With an adult, prepare the recipe and serve it to a friend or family member.

Chicken Pot Pie: Read 100 pages about birds. You may read fiction or non-fiction. You may read one, 100 page chapter book or three picture books. You may read about chickens, penguins, ducks, or any other kind of bird.

Desserts

Fudge Sundae: Three scoops of something delicious. Read any three picture books or stories that you find delightful.

Carrot Cake: Tall, nutty, and sweet. Read a long, funny story. A book about 100 pages in length will be just right.

Strawberries and Cream: A bowl full of sweet little bites. Read seven poems, three picture books, or a whole page of newspaper comic strips.

My Reading Goals: _____

_____

_____

_____

_____

Name: _____ Age: _____

Sample Reading Menu

Teddy Bear Picnic

For many children, a teddy bear is a beloved friend. This program provides children with an opportunity to show off their bear and see the many sizes, costumes, and colors of other teddy bears. Children are given the chance to speak in front of others, practice social skills, and increase their awareness of other places in the world.

Description of Program

Invite children to bring a teddy bear of their own to this program. The story area can be decorated with picnic blankets on the floor, picnic baskets, flowers, and other green plants. If you like, a world map or globe can be placed in view. Children may be given a teddy bear nametag (pattern on p. 10) to wear at the program. Provide 20 minutes of bear stories and songs, then invite the children to show and tell something about their teddy bear. As each bear is presented, the children can show the bear's origin on a map or globe. If the place is not known, then a place that the bear would like to visit someday can be shown.

Some questions to facilitate the show and tell:

> Was this bear a gift?
> What is your bear's name?
> Where is your bear's favorite reading place?
> Is your bear afraid of anything?
> Where is your bear ticklish?

Then ask three children to bring their bears forward. Questions can be asked which help the children compare and contrast the sizes, colors, and costumes of the bears.

> Which bear is tallest?
> Which bear has the longest hair?
> Which bear is wearing a hat?
> Are all of the bears the same color? What colors are they?

Give teddy bear cookies to the children at the end of the program.

For Ages: 2–6

Length: 30 minutes

Limit: 30 children

Staff or volunteer requirements: Two adults, or one adult and one young adult

Volunteer assignments: Decorate the story area. Arrange the teddy bear collection display. Assist with handing out cookies to the children.

Preparation time: 1–2 hours.

Preparation: Select stories and songs or contact storyteller. Purchase teddy bear cookies. Collect decorations for story area. Arrange to borrow teddy bear collection.

Supplies needed: Teddy bear-shaped cookies, picnic blankets and baskets for decorations, globe or world map.

Community resources needed: Teddy bear collection for display *(optional)*.

Read More About It

Aylesworth, Jim. *Teddy Bear Tears.* Atheneum. 1997. Each of four teddy bears fears something at bedtime, and as their young master explains away each fear, he makes the night worry-free for himself, too.

Sheldon, Dyan. *Love, Your Bear, Pete.* Candlewick Press, 1994. Although she misses her stuffed bear after he is left behind on the bus, a young girl enjoys the postcards he sends her from all the faraway places he visits. Older children will enjoy finding the faraway places on a world map or globe.

Waddell, Martin. *Small Bear Lost.* Candlewick Press, 1996. A girl leaves Small Bear, her teddy bear, on the train, but he finds his way home after many adventures.

Waddell, Martin. *When the Teddy Bears Came.* Candlewick Press, 1994. When Tom's mother brings home the new baby, so many teddy bears arrive as gifts that there is no room for Tom, but she assures him that there will always be a place for him.

My name is _____

My bear's name is

_____

Teddy Bear Nametag Pattern

Gingerbread Day

An old-fashioned art form that is still appreciated today is the gingerbread house. No need to save this program for winter holidays. It can be just as much fun to do in the summer. This program allows children to try their hand at culinary arts, and work together to create a masterpiece that can be displayed in the library.

Description of Program

Invite children to decorate a gingerbread house for display. This is a team effort, lead by a cake decorator. Children discuss and decide where to put various candies and take turns applying them to the gingerbread house.

Another way to do this program is to provide a gingerbread cookie for each child, which they will decorate and take home with them. The cake decorator demonstrates techniques for applying the frosting and decorating with candies.

You can order undecorated gingerbread houses or cookies from a bakery, or prepare the gingerbread yourself.

For a literacy connection, you can read a story to the children before beginning the project. Two excellent and recent versions of the classic gingerbread man folktale are included in the "Read More About It" section at right.

You may also give children a paper gingerbread person to decorate at home, extending the program to include an additional medium, and allowing another opportunity for creativity. A pattern for this activity appears on p. 12.

For ages: 7–10

Length: 60 minutes

Limit: 20 children

Staff or volunteer requirements: One adult or one young adult

Volunteer assignments: Assist children at the program, under the direction of the baker. Help with cleaning hands and tools from time to time, and assist with clean-up when the project is completed.

Preparation time: 1 hour

Preparation: Arrange for a baker to lead the program. Purchase baked gingerbread cookies or house and decorating supplies. Cover tables with plastic or newspaper.

Supplies needed: One baked, undecorated gingerbread house or one baked, undecorated gingerbread cookie per child; frosting; decorating tools; variety of candies; paper towels

Community resources: Baker or cake decorator, either a professional or a skilled amateur (*optional*).

Read More About It

Aylesworth, Jim. *The Gingerbread Man.* Scholastic, 1998. A freshly baked gingerbread man escapes when he is taken out of the oven.

Brett, Jan. *Gingerbread Baby.* Putnam, 1999. When Matti opens the oven door, out pops a gingerbread baby! He taunts Matti's parents, a cat, the goats, and he even outwits the fox.

Currie, Christa. *Gingerbread Houses: A Complete Guide to Baking, Building and Decorating.* Doubleday, 1994. This step-by-step guide includes patterns, recipes, and decorating guides for the beginning or experienced gingerbread house baker.

My Gingerbread Person

Name: _____

Zucchini Whambini

What do you do when summer vegetable gardens produce bushels of zucchini? It's the perfect time to play with your food! This program provides art activities, games, and cooking practice for the whole family. A festival atmosphere is created, with several activities happening throughout the day. Measuring distances, reading recipes, and creating and naming characters are all educational activities.

Description of Program

At this event, up to four activities may be offered. These include a zucchini dress-up contest that involves letting participants use fabric scraps, felt, etc. to dress their zucchini as a character. Participants should give their character a name, such as "Zucchini Penguini" for a penguin. Zucchini costumes may be animals (Zucchini Catteeny), book characters (Harry Potter, Wizard Zucchini), family members (Zucchini Baby), professionals (Doctor Zuke), or an original character (Squash Monster). Awards should be given for best name, best costume, funniest zucchini, etc. Trophies or certificates can be awarded (see p. 14). The Home-grown Zucchini Contest is an opportunity for gardeners to show off their harvest. Awards can be given for the heaviest squash, longest squash, curliest squash, ugliest squash, etc. The Zucchini Toss is an athletic competition. From a designated spot, participants throw zucchini by hand or launch them by catapult into a field. The distance is measured after each toss. The award goes to the longest distance. You must have permission to make a mess, since broken pieces of squash will be scattered across the field. It will be tremendous fun, and worth the trouble. The Zucchini Bake-off allows families to show off their favorite zucchini recipes. Tasting can be allowed after the awards are given. Complete the event by having food vendors provide lunch for sale, if desired.

For ages: All

Length: 60–90 minutes

Limit: No limit to number of children

Staff and volunteer requirements: Three to five adults or young adults —varies with size of event

Volunteer assignments: Assist children with decorating zucchini, measure and mark distances for zucchini toss, provide crowd control, judge bake-off contest, home-grown zucchini contest and zucchini dress-up contest.

Preparation time: 2–3 hours

Preparation: Purchase zucchini in quantity. Gather supplies for decorating the zucchini. Make certificates or order ribbons for awards. Arrange for a place to hold the zucchini toss outdoors. Publicize the event.

Supplies needed: A large number of zucchini of various sizes (about 3 per person), fabric scraps, feathers, felt, buttons, trims, paper, straight pins, white glue, trophies, certificates or ribbons

Community resources needed: Use of a park or open field for zucchini toss; local celebrities for judges *(optional)*.

Read More About It

Elffers, Joost. *Play with Your Food.* Stewart Tabori & Chang, 1997. Photos of unusual and creative vegetable sculptures.

Freymann, Saxton. *How Are You Peeling: Foods with Moods.* Arthur A. Levine Books, 1999. Brief text and photographs of carvings made from vegetables introduce the world of emotions.

Ralston, Nancy. *The New Zucchini Cookbook.* Storey Communications, 1990. 170 pages of recipes using the prolific zucchini.

Zucchini Whambini Award

presented to:

_____

For outstanding zucchini:

_____

_____ _____
signed   date

Zucchini Whambini Award pattern

Tea and Crumpets: Etiquette Tea

The days of white gloves and party dresses can be revived and given a decidedly up-to-date slant. Although society is generally more casual now than in former decades, it still is important for every young person to learn proper table manners, acceptable dinner conversation, and what to do with those elbows.

Description of Program

Invite children to come dressed in their best for this program. (See sample invitation on p. 16.) Prepare light snacks with the children, such as spreadable cheese and crackers or simple sandwiches. Before the adults serve the tea and snacks, instruct children in proper table etiquette. A puppet makes a good instructor, and the instructions can certainly be light-hearted and funny. This should be a gentle introduction to the art of elegant dining, polite conversation, and party manners. It may be possible to find a maitre d' from a fine restaurant in your area who will be a good host for the party, and is willing to offer some tips on proper restaurant manners, such as what to do with the napkin, which fork to use when, and proper posture. It is best to keep the children close in age, but the program can be repeated, so that two age groups can be accommodated one right after the other on the same day.

For ages: 2–5 or 6–10

Length: 60 minutes

Limit: 20 children

Staff or volunteer requirements: Two adults, one may be a parent or community volunteer

Preparation time: 2–3 hours

Preparation: Contact area restaurants to find a host and arrange for tableware. Register the children for the program, and send them an invitation in the mail. Purchase snack foods. Set up a stereo and soft background music. Set table and decorate the room. Prepare brief remarks about table manners, proper dinner conversation, and restaurant etiquette, or ask an expert to present this.

Supplies needed: Pretty tableware; holiday decorations (*optional*); light snacks that can be prepared by the children; tea or other beverage; background music

Community resources needed: Antiques for display from a private source or a store (*optional*); a host from one of your area's nicest restaurants (*optional*)

Read More About It

Buehner, Caralyn. *It's a Spoon, Not a Shovel.* Dial Books for Young Readers, 1995. Humorous questions and answers about etiquette for children and teenagers.

Polisar, Barry. *Don't Do That!: A Child's Guide to Bad Manners, Ridiculous Rules, and Inadequate Etiquette.* Rainbow Morning, 1995. A humorous introduction to good manners and behavior in relation to home and school activities.

Wallace, Carol. *Elbows Off the Table, Napkin in the Lap, No Video Games During Dinner: The Modern Guide to Teaching Children Good Manners.* St. Martin's Press, 1996. A fun guide to etiquette for children and teenagers in today's society.

Ziegler, Sandra. *The Child's World of Manners.* Child's World, 1997. Provides suggestions for practicing manners in various social situations.

You are cordially invited to attend an

Etiquette Tea

Date: _____

Time: _____

Place: _____

Dress in your best. Refreshments will be served.

Sample Etiquette Tea invitation

Yankee Noodle Day

"Yankee Doodle went to town, riding on a pony. He stuck a feather in his hat and called it macaroni!" This well-known song names one of the most familiar varieties of pasta. Pasta, meaning "paste or dough" in Italian, has been a favorite food of people around the world for a long time. It is made from wheat flour, which is mixed with water and sometimes other ingredients, such as eggs, green spinach, herbs, or tomatoes. Then, it is rolled and cut into many interesting shapes. Put on a program that introduces children to the pasta-making process and the great variety of pasta shapes.

Description of Program

As an introduction to the program, read a storybook that includes pasta. Then, demonstrate the process of making pasta with a pasta machine. Give the children a variety of pasta shapes, markers, paper, and glue and ask them to create a collage. An educational game sheet, "Pasta Shapes," can be given as a take home project, or it can be done together as a group. (See p. 18.) If desired, serve a snack of prepared pasta.

For ages: 5 and up

Length: 45 minutes

Limit: 30 children

Staff or volunteer requirements: One adult and one young adult

Volunteer assignments: Assist with setting up the room. Assist with passing out the paper and markers to the children, and setting out the pasta varieties. Assist with handing out the prepared pasta.

Preparation time: 1–2 hours

Preparation: Select a story to read. Contact someone to bring in a pasta machine, and demonstrate how it works. This can be someone from your organization's staff, or someone from a store that sells pasta machines. Make copies of the Pasta Shapes hand-out. Purchase a variety of shapes and colors of pasta for the collage. Collect enough paper, glue, and markers for the children to use in making the collage. Order prepared pasta to be delivered at the time of the program for tasting, (*optional*).

Supplies needed: 9x12" paper for each child, white glue, assorted shapes and colors of pasta, markers

Community resources needed: Pasta machine and someone to demonstrate how it works and prepared pasta for tasting (*optional*)

Read More About It

DePaola, Tomie. *Strega Nona, Her Story*. Putnam, 1996. Grandma Concetta heals everyone with her remedies and advice. When she retires, she leaves Strega Nona her magic pasta pot with its secret ingredient.

DePaola, Tomie. *Strega Nona*. Prentice-Hall, 1975. When Strega Nona leaves him alone with her magic pasta pot, Big Anthony shows the townspeople how it works.

Egan, Robert. *From Wheat to Pasta: A Photo Essay*. Children's Press, 1997. With text and photographs, the steps in making various kinds of pasta are shown, from growing wheat to shaping the final product.

Machotka, Hana. *Pasta Factory*. Houghton Mifflin, 1992. Children see how noodles are made at the Tutta Pasta factory.

Pasta Shapes

Draw a line from the name for each pasta shape
to the correct drawing.

Alphabets

Wagon Wheels

Angel Hair

Jumbo Shells

Rotini

Macaroni

Egg Noodles

Bow Ties

Lasagna

Penne

Orzo

Fettuccine

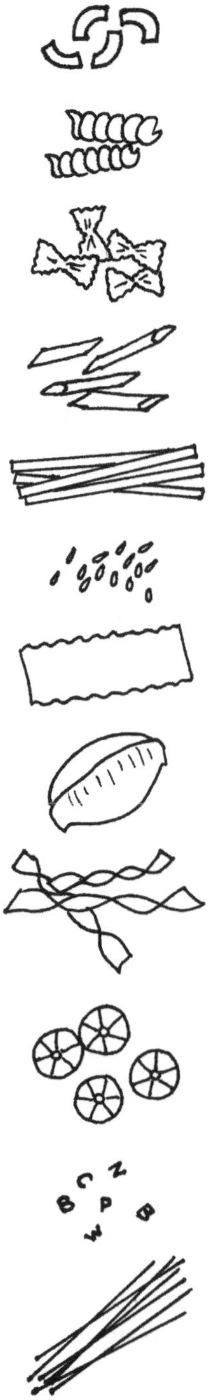

One Potato, Two Potato

Potatoes are a versatile vegetable, and one that most children enjoy. This program shows children how potatoes grow and allows them to create a print using potatoes.

Description of Program

Show the children a potato, pointing out the eye, and show a sprouted potato, explaining how potatoes grow. Two books that have been illustrated with potato prints are included in the "Read More About It" section that follows. You can show the children some examples of the beautiful illustrations. Then, if desired, read a story containing potatoes. Finally, with potatoes that have been pre-cut for stamping, have the children make a potato print picture.

For ages: 3 and up

Length: 30 minutes

Limit: 30 children

Staff or volunteer requirements: Two adults

Volunteer assignments: Cover work tables with newspapers. Set out pie plates filled with tempera paints. Cut the potato shapes before the program. Keep them moist in plastic bags until time for use.

Preparation time: 1 hour

Preparation: Select a book or two to share with the children. Set up tables for potato printing. Purchase potatoes and cut—or ask a volunteer to cut—one half potato for each child into a simple stamp (see instructions at right). Buy or borrow several pie plates, purchase several colors of tempera paint, and enough 9x12" sheets of construction paper for each child.

Supplies needed: 15 to 20 potatoes, variety of tempera paints, paring knife, newspapers for covering tables, construction paper, sprouted potato for visual aid

Craft: Potato Prints

Before the Program: Select firm potatoes with smooth skins. Cut potatoes in half lengthwise. Wipe the face of the potato with a cotton cloth.

Begin by creating simple geometric shapes on paper or use the shapes provided on p. 20. Place each shape on a cut potato. Trace around the shape with a pencil, making an indentation. Then, using a paring knife, cut the outline, then cut away the rest of the potato, leaving the shape to stand alone. You should cut about half an inch deep all around the shape.

During the Program: Children dip the potato into thick tempera paint, then place it face down on the paper, putting even pressure on the potato with their hand. They lift the potato and reveal the print. Have them try overlapping the shape with different colors, or use several shapes to create a pleasing design. They must wipe off the potato with a paper towel before printing with a new color, to keep the colors pure. In addition to stamping on paper, they can stamp on fabric, such as T-shirts, pillowcases or scarves using fabric paints.

Read More About It

Creasy, Rosalind. *Blue Potatoes, Orange Tomatoes: How to Grow a Rainbow Garden.* Sierra Club Books for Children, 1994. Describes how to plant and grow a variety of colorful vegetables.

Davis, Aubrey. *The Enormous Potato.* Kids Can Press, 1998. A farmer's potato grows to such an enormous size that he needs lots of help to pull it up.

Pomeroy, Diana. *One Potato: A Counting Book of Potato Prints.* Harcourt Brace, 1996. A counting book which uses images of fruits and vegetables to illustrate numbers. Also includes an explanation of how to do potato printing.

Pomeroy, Diana. *Wildflower ABC: An Alphabet of Potato Prints.* Harcourt Brace, 1997. Presents potato print illustrations of wildflowers for every letter of the alphabet.

Shiefman, Vicky. *Sunday Potatoes, Monday Potatoes.* Simon & Schuster, 1994. A poor family eats potatoes each day of the week except on Saturday, when they eat their special potato pudding. Recipe is included.

Potato Print Patterns

Creating Cornelia: Corn Husk Dolls

Corn husk dolls have long been associated with harvest time in many countries. In England, farmers in remote areas carried out ceremonies at harvest time, including the making of corn husk dolls, right up to the early twentieth century. The tradition was carried to the new world, and American pioneers handed down the art form from generation to generation. Some villages celebrated the triumphant return of the last load of corn with a parade down the main street, the corn husk doll held in the arms of one of the village girls. It was hung in her house until the next year. Pioneer children practiced the art of making corn husk dolls, because in those days toys were all handmade.

Description of Program

Children create a corn husk doll to take home. (See sample on p. 22.) You may want to dress in a pioneer costume. Corn stalks or dried corn on the cob can be displayed in the room. A florist or crafter skilled in corn husk creations may display their work, if desired. Before beginning the dolls, discuss with the children the importance of corn as a staple food crop in their community and in other cultures. Several books are listed in the "Read More About It" section on p. 22, for reading to the children or for use as background information. Serve popcorn as a treat at the end of the program.

For ages: 6 and up

Length: 60 minutes

Limit: 30 children

Staff or volunteer requirements: One adult presenter and one volunteer

Volunteer assignments: Decorate the room with corn stalks or dried corn on the cob. Separate the corn husks, and put them in a tub of water to soak. Assist the children with tying and constructing their dolls.

Preparation time: 1–2 hours

Preparation: Select books to read, or prepare a few minutes of discussion about corn. Purchase corn husks, and assemble the other materials needed. Make a corn husk doll to show to the children before they begin. You may wish to make a boy doll and a girl doll to show.

Supplies needed: Corn husks for making tamales, found in grocery store, or shucked from sweet corn and allowed to dry; white glue; small pieces of dress materials; styrofoam cups; rubber bands; felt-tipped pens; small sharp scissors; pan of water for soaking corn husks; lanolin, found at drug store; paper towels; twine or cotton string

Community resources needed: Florist or crafter skilled in corn husk creations, (*optional*). This person may teach the craft also, or it may be taught by the program planner or the volunteer.

Craft: Corn Husk Dolls

1. Thirty to sixty minutes before the program, soak the corn husks in a dish pan or other tub, adding a few drops of lanolin to the water to aid in softening them.

2. When ready to make dolls, remove 8–10 husks from the water, and pat dry on paper towels.

3. Tie four or five husks together, 2" from the narrow end. This is the top.

4. Fold over, hiding the ends inside. Tie the neck with twine or a rubber band.

5. Roll two large husks into a pencil shape. Insert it between the husks bellow the neck, extending a few inches on each side. This forms the arms.

6. Tie the waist below the arms with twine or rubber band. Tie the wrists, and trim the ends of the arms with scissors, forming the hands.

For a girl doll: Add aprons or more skirts with corn husks or cloth. Shape the skirt over a styrofoam cup, and allow the doll to dry.

For a boy doll: Divide the husks in half, forming two legs. Tie the ankles. Trim the ends, forming the feet.

When dry enough, add features using cloth, glue, and felt tipped pens. Hats and other clothing can be created from husks or cloth. Hair can be added using corn silk, twine, or braided corn husks.

Read More About It

Kalman, Bobbie. *Pioneer Projects.* Crabtree, 1997. This book presents instructions for handicrafts and activities from pioneer days.

Saunders-Smith, Gail. *Fall Harvest.* Pebble Books, 1998. Simple text and photographs describe how several different crops are harvested.

Gerson, Mary-Joan. *People Of Corn: A Mayan Story.* Little Brown, 1995. After several unsuccessful attempts to create grateful creatures, the Mayan gods use sacred corn to fashion a people who will thank and praise their creators.

Kettleman, Helen. *The Year of No More Corn.* Orchard Books, 1993. Beanie's grandfather tells him about the failure of the corn crop in 1928 and how he was able to make corn trees grow from whittled corn kernels.

Sample corn husk dolls

Milk Money Service Project

Children are interested in helping others and making the world a better place to live. This program provides children with an opportunity to experience working together to achieve a goal, practice creativity, and increase their awareness of the needs of others.

Description of Program

Children decorate small milk cartons which will be used as collection banks to raise money for a shelter or food bank in your community. First, they create posters for display in the community to create awareness and interest in this project. Then, on a designated day, children create their banks and posters with materials that you provide. When each child is finished creating his or her bank, give them a Milk Money nametag to wear as they distribute the banks. (See sample on p. 23.) During the designated collection time, place banks around the community in businesses that have agreed to participate. This will allow the public to donate spare change which will be donated to the shelter or food bank. Place some banks at the circulation desk of the library, and explain the project to patrons as they check out books. Where possible, hang posters which have been created by the children that explain the project. At the end of the project, collect the banks. Take the change to the bank to be counted, and ask for a cashier's check made out in the name of your charity. Inform the public how much money was raised with posters in the library or an ad in the local newspaper.

For ages: All

Length: Two or three hours on a designated day to create the banks and posters. The project can last for several weeks or for the duration of your reading program.

Limit: No limit on the number of participants

Staff or volunteer requirements: One adult to coordinate the program. One or two adults or young adults to assist with the banks and posters.

Preparation time: 1–2 hours

Preparation: Ask a school to save milk cartons from school lunch. You will need to estimate the number needed. Clean and dry the milk cartons, and cut a coin slot in the top. Staple the top of the carton closed. Make labels to attach to the posters, explaining the project. Contact a food bank or shelter, and explain the project several weeks before you begin. Discuss their needs, and agree on how the money should be handled. Purchase and gather the materials for decorating the banks and making the posters.

Materials needed for banks: Milk cartons, construction paper, glue, rubber stamps and stamp pads, markers, colored pencils, crayons

Materials needed for posters: 9 x 12" sheets of construction paper or poster board, drawing materials, and prepared labels to attach to the posters (pattern provided on p.24).

Read More About It

Bunting, Eve. *December.* Harcourt Brace, 1997. A homeless family's luck changes after they help an old woman who has even less than they do.

Raatma, Lucia. *Caring.* Bridgestone Books, 2000. Describes "caring" as a virtue and suggests ways in which it can be shown, such as recycling, donating to charity, helping others and listening.

Spaide, Deborah. *Teaching Your Kids to Care: How to Discover and Develop the Spirit of Charity in Your Children.* Carol Publishing Group, 1995. Discusses ways to motivate children to give to charity and be willing to volunteer to help others.

Wittlinger, Ellen. *Gracie's Girl.* Simon and Schuster, 2000. Bess volunteers to work on the school musical in hopes of fitting in, but when she and a friend get to know an elderly homeless woman, she changes her mind about what is really important.

Service project nametag pattern

Milk Money Service Project
Help us feed the hungry!
The children at _____
are collecting spare change to be donated to:
_____.
Dates of the project: _____

Sample service project label

2 Reading Round-up

The cowboy era of the west has wide appeal. This theme should round up plenty of young buckaroos! The programs are varied and fun for children of all ages. Some are active programs, such as the Bicycle Rodeo. Some are high-interest programs, like the Baby Animals Fair. Some are western crafts, and some are science programs. Decorate the library with bales of hay, ropes, cowboy hats, and bandannas. You may even corral some toy horses, cattle, and sheep for a display. Book displays can include such subject as rodeos, horsemanship, western wildlife, and pioneer life.

Since many children are fond of horses, the service project for this program encourages children to sponsor a wild mustang by reading books. The awards for reaching the reading goal can be requested from restaurants, petting zoos, and western wear stores. You may purchase pencils for prizes in denim color, or imprinted with horses. You may give bandannas or cowboy hats as special awards. A chuck wagon bar-b-cue party could be given at the end of the program to celebrate reaching the reading goal.

A western trail map-style reading record is provided on p. 26. Children color in objects along the trail as they read. Children should select a reading goal according to their age and reading level.

Reading Round-Up!

Name _____ Age _____

Draw a lasso around your reading level brand.

Level 1: Read or listen to 3 picture books

Level 2: Read 100 pages

Each time you read your reading level brand, color in an object on the trail below. When you reach the end of the trail, show the map to your librarian.

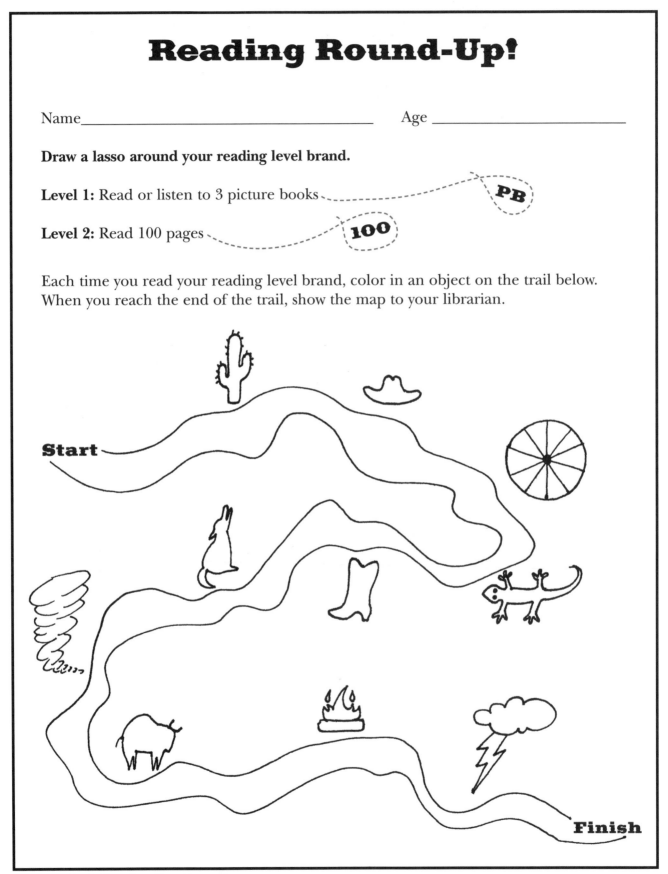

Western Trail Map Reading Record

Urban Cowboy Bicycle Rodeo

Long ago, a child's transportation was a horse. Today it is carpools, school buses, roller blades and bicycles. In the spirit of the old western rodeo, this program provides children with an opportunity to show their bike-riding skills in a friendly competition, and it offers the opportunity to remind kids about bicycle safety.

Description of Program

There are three stations to the rodeo: the riding course, the safety inspection, and the story corner. The riding course and safety inspection are conducted by the police department. Encourage participants to dress in western wear, and play country music, either live or recorded, for a festive touch.

Invite children to ride their bicycles through an obstacle course set up in the parking lot or basketball court.

Have their bicycles inspected for safety, and instruct the children in safe riding practices, the necessity for wearing helmets, and proper etiquette when riding on pedestrian trails.

A story corner inside the library is the final station. If you have more children than can be accommodated in one story session, a new session can begin every 15 minutes, as children complete the outdoor activities. At the end of the story session, give the children a certificate of completion. (See sample on p. 28.)

For ages: 6 and up

Length: 60–90 minutes

Staff of volunteer requirements: One adult in the story corner, and one other adult

Volunteer assignments: Write children's names on certificates at the end of the story session.

Community resources needed: Two or three officers from the local police department

Entertainer needed: Western music *(optional)*

Preparation time: 1 hour

Preparation: Contact the police department, and arrange for their assistance with the program. Contact an entertainer to provide music, or arrange for recorded music to be played outdoors. Select stories to be read at the story corner. Make copies of the certificates.

Read More About It

Brett, Jan. *Armadillo Rodeo*. Putnam, 1995. Bo, the armadillo, rides a bronco, eats red-hot chile peppers, and tries the two-step at the rodeo.

Brown, Marc. *D.W. Rides Again!* Little Brown, 1993. D.W. graduates from a tricycle to her first two-wheeler.

Loewen, Nancy. *Bicycle Safety*. Child's World Press, 1996. Explains the safe way to ride a bicycle and identifies important equipment such as the helmet, reflectors, and basket.

Rice, James. *Cowboy Rodeo*. Gretna, Pelican Publishing, 1992. Describes the atmosphere and the events of the rodeo in its early days.

Bicycle Rodeo Award

presented to:

_____

For completing the bicycle rodeo riding course
and safety check, and for being a safe rider!

_____   _____
signed   date

Bicycle Rodeo Award pattern

Desert Flower Pots

Growing plants in containers can be challenging and fun. This craft program provides children with an opportunity to be creative, and will provide them with a beautiful container for their garden.

Description of Program

After hearing some stories about deserts and gardening, and a brief discussion of container gardening, children stencil a design on the outside of a 6" terra-cotta flower pot. The craft area should have table space to accommodate the children. The tables should be covered with newspapers or table clothes to protect them from paint. The children should wear paint shirts or aprons to protect their clothing.

For ages: 6 and up

Length: 45 minutes

Limit: 30 children

Staff or volunteer requirements: One adult and one young adult volunteer

Volunteer assignments: Cut stencils before the program. Spread newspapers on the tables before the program. Assist with stenciling the pots. Help with clean-up.

Preparation time: 1–2 hours

Preparation: Purchase supplies. Supervise the cutting of the stencils. Select a book to read, and prepare a brief discussion on container gardening. Prepare to discuss the kinds of plants that grow in a desert.

Supplies needed: 6" Terra-cotta pot with saucer for each child; acrylic paints in green, rust, yellow, brown, other earth tones; pie pans; stencil brushes; sponges; manila folders for cutting the stencils; craft knife or exact-o knife; masking tape

Craft: Desert Flower Pots

Cut stencils on 4" square pieces of manila folders, using the designs on p. 30. You will need at least one stencil per child, which will be traded and used several times. At the program, show the children how to tape the stencil to the pot with masking tape. Using a stencil brush or sponge, the children should apply a small amount of paint over the stencil. The brush or sponge should be almost dry, for best results. The stencil can be repositioned and taped in place again, or a different stencil can be taped to the pot, but care must be taken not to smear the previously painted area. The new stencil should be painted as the previous one was. The saucer can be painted, if desired. When the pot is complete, the children are encouraged to take it home and use it to grow a container garden.

Suggested desert plants for small containers:

- Prickly Pear Cactus
- Aloe Vera
- Pincushion Cactus

Suggested non-desert plants for small containers:

- Marigold
- Moss Rose
- Asparagus Fern

Read More About It

Allard, Harry. *The Cactus Flower Bakery*. HarperCollins, 1991. A near-sighted armadillo meets a snake in the desert and helps her open a bakery.

Bunting, Eve. *Flower Garden*. Harcourt Brace Jovanovich, 1994. Helped by her father, a young girl prepares a flower garden as a birthday surprise for her mother.

Colburn, Nigel. *The Container Garden*. Crescent Books, 1995. Instructions for planting and caring for container gardens.

Cole, Rebecca. *Potted Gardens: A Fresh Approach to Container Gardening*. Clarkson Potter, 1997. Provides gardening tips for container gardens, and suggests many kinds of containers to use for container gardens.

Walheim, Lance. *Best Kids Garden Book*. Sunset, 1992. Detailed instructions and illustrations showing how to plant and grow all kinds of gardens, including container gardens.

flower pot stencil patterns

Baby Animals Fair

There is nothing more appealing to young children than a kitten, a lamb, or a piglet. This program allows children to see, hear, and touch baby animals, and learn about the habits of various animals. They may bring a toy animal to the program, which encourages their participation.

Description of Program

Ask a farmer, pet store owner, animal shelter worker or library patron who owns animals to bring a variety of baby animals to show. If it is not possible to arrange for live animals, a variety of toy animals may be displayed in a pretend petting zoo. The children wear special nametags (see p. 32 for pattern). You or the visitor talks about what baby animals are called, what they eat, where they sleep, and how they avoid danger. Share some books with photos of animals with the children, and allow them to pet the animals. Each child may show the toy animal he or she brought, and tell the group something about the animal. Play the word game, "Baby, Baby."

For ages: 3–5

Length: 30 minutes

Limit: 30 children

Staff of volunteer requirements: One adult

Preparation time: 1 hour

Preparation: Select books to read. Contact someone to bring animals to show. Make name tags for each child from the pattern included, (*optional*).

Community resources needed: Someone to bring baby animals

Game: "Baby, Baby"

Ask the children to act like or make a noise like baby animals. Then have them complete the sentence which identifies the baby animal. Some suggestions are:

Can you squeal like a piglet? A piglet is a baby __.
Can you hop like a joey? A joey is a baby __.
Can you gallop like a foal? A foal is a baby __.
Can you bleat like a lamb? A lamb is a baby __.

Read More About It

Darling, Kathy. *Desert Babies*. Walker, 1997. Photographs and brief text describe a variety of baby animals who make their homes in the desert.

Donahue, Dorothy. *Big and Little on the Farm*. Golden Books, 1999. Children will learn the names of adult and baby animals they meet on each page.

Maynard, Christopher. *Amazing Animal Babies*. Knopf, 1993. Introduces a variety of baby animals, discusses how they learn, feed, grow, and survive.

Baby animal nametag patterns

This Little Piggy

Pigs are intelligent animals! This program provides children with an opportunity to learn about pigs through books and a word search game. It also gives them a chance to create a tiny pig from a peanut.

Description of Program

Introduce children to the characteristics of pigs, where they live, what they eat, and what they provide for people through fiction and non-fiction books. Give the children a copy of the word search to complete as you ask them questions (see p. 34). Then give the children some peanuts and supplies to create a tiny pig to take home.

For ages: 6 and up

Length: 45 minutes

Limit: 30 children

Staff or volunteer requirements: One adult

Preparation time: 1 hour

Preparation: Purchase supplies for the craft. Make copies of the word search. Select books to read.

Supplies needed: Tacky glue; peanuts in the shell; un-popped popcorn for ears and feet; tiny, two-hole buttons for nose; tiny beads for eyes; pipe cleaners for tail; scissors to cut pipe cleaners; toothpicks, for curling tail

Craft: Peanut Pigs

Following the illustration, glue ears, eyes, nose, and feet to peanut with tacky craft glue. Curl a 2" length of pipe cleaner around a toothpick to form tail. Glue the curled pipe cleaner to the pig.

Read More About It

Blackstone, Stella and Clare Beaton. *How Big Is A Pig?* Barefoot Books, 2000. Follow the trail of animal opposites through the farmyard to the biggest pig of all. Rhyming text.

Casey, Patricia. *Beep! Beep! Oink! Oink! Animals in the City.* Candlewick Press, 1997. All kinds of animals, including pigeons, pigs, cats and chickens, can be found living in the city.

Fries, Claudia. *A Pig Is Moving In!* Orchard Books, 2000. Dr. Fox, Henrietta Hen and Nick Hare are worried when a pig moves into their building, but they are pleasantly surprised to find out he is a good neighbor.

Swan, Erin Pembrey. *Camels and Pigs: What They Have In Common.* F. Watts, 1999. Describes members of the order of animals that have hooves with an even number of toes.

Peanut pig

Pig Word Search

Find and circle the words listed below. They may read across, up, or down.

```
S O M E P I G K M R
A L G R A I N N U D
P I G L E T S I D R
B A T H B E C O N U
T T P W O I N K J B
U L E N A U V A G L
O D N T R O U G H I
N P H U M B L S O W
S M A R T B P I G S
```

1. bath	6. pen	11. some pig
2. boar	7. piglets	12. sow
3. grain	8. pigs	13. tail
4. mud	9. smart	14. trough
5. oink	10. snout	15. Wilbur

Make Your Own Tornado

Weather is fascinating because it is so powerful. In the west, tornadoes are common. This program helps children understand how tornadoes are formed and allows them to experience the power of tornadoes through stories and activities.

Description of Program

Read a selection of fiction or non-fiction books about tornadoes. Then, discuss with the children how tornadoes are formed and how to keep safe during a tornado. The children then create a tornado in a bottle, which gives them a visual image of what a tornado looks like.

For ages: 7 and up

Length: 30 minutes

Limit: 30 children

Staff or volunteer requirements: One adult

Preparation time: 1 hour

Preparation: Collect clear plastic soda bottles, one for each child. Purchase supplies. Select the books to read, and prepare to discuss them.

Supplies needed: Clear, 2-liter soda bottle with lid for each child; water; teaspoon of salt for each bottle; drop of dishwashing detergent for each bottle; food color (*optional*); small plastic houses, figures, and cars (*optional*).

Craft: Tornado in a Bottle

Fill the bottle with water, leaving one inch of air at the top. Add one teaspoon of salt. Put on the cap. Shake until salt is dissolved. Add a drop of dishwashing detergent, and a drop of food color if desired. Do not shake. Add two or three small figures, including a house or a car, if desired.

To see the tornado work, put the cap on the bottle tightly. Move the bottle, while in an upright position, in clockwise direction. A vortex will form in the fluid. A vortex is a spiral motion. In a real tornado, the vortex forms in the air.

Read More About It

Beard, Darleen Bailey. *Twister.* Farrar Straus Giroux, 1999. Two children experience a tornado.

Byars, Betsy. *Tornado.* HarperCollins, 1996. As they wait out a tornado in their storm cellar, a family listens to their farmhand tell stories about the dog that was blown into his life by another tornado when he was a boy.

Christian, Spencer. *Can It Really Rain Frogs? The World's Strangest Weather Events.* Wiley, 1997. Describes strange weather events and discusses weather lore and weather forecasting.

Hooker, Merrilee. *Tornadoes.* Rourke, 1993. Discusses how tornadoes begin and work, and gives safety advice.

Desert Lizards

If you have been lucky enough to see a lizard in its natural habitat, you may have only gotten a quick glance. Most lizards are very fast, which helps them keep safe from predators, such as birds and coyotes. This program introduces children to some characteristics of lizards and allows them to see and touch some. The children make a Gila Monster finger puppet to take home.

Description of Program

Discuss the characteristics of lizards. A reptile owner from the community can show one or more live lizards. The children play an educational game called, "Hibernate," then they make a Gila Monster finger puppet to take home. (See p. 36.)

Some facts to share about lizards:

1. Lizards are reptiles, as are snakes, alligators, and turtles.

2. Lizards are cold blooded, and must get heat from warm surroundings.

3. Some lizards can change their color.

4. Most lizards have moveable eyelids and ear openings.

5. Lizards do not feel slimy. They are covered with scales, and may feel smooth or rough.

6. Lizards have good vision and sense of smell. Some lizards smell with their tongues.

7. Gila Monsters have a poisonous bite. They live in Arizona and other western states.

8. In cold climates, lizards hibernate 8 or 9 months of the year, and are only active in May, June, July and August.

For ages: 5 and up

Length: 45 minutes

Limit: 30 children

Staff or volunteer requirements: One adult leader and one young adult to help with the craft.

Volunteer assignments: Cut out lizards before the program. Cut index cards, and make the finger tubes before the program. Assist children with gluing and assembling the craft during the program.

Preparation time: 2 hours

Preparation: Invite a zoo worker, pet store owner or patron who owns lizards to show their animals at the program. Purchase the supplies. Prepare the craft materials. Prepare a discussion about lizards from the outline at left. Select lizard books to display. Lead the "Hibernation" game.

Game: "Hibernate"

Post a list of months during which lizards in cold climates are active. The children sit on the floor in a circle. One child is selected to be "It." The rest of the children are Lizards. "It" walks around the circle, touching each "Lizard" on the head and naming the months, in random order. The Lizards are still until they hear an "active" month named. When a Lizard is touched and one of the active months is named, he gets up and chase "It" around the circle, racing him back to his place. The first child to sit becomes a Lizard, and the other child is "It." The game continues for a specific amount of time. About 10 minutes is good.

Craft Project: Gila Monster Finger Puppet

Supplies needed: Brown paper bags; pink and black tiny beads; white glue; 3x5" index cards, cut to 1½" x 2½"; tiny wiggle eyes

Before the Program: Using the pattern included, cut out a Gila Monster for each child from brown paper bags or other stiff paper. Cut the index cards into quarters, then roll each cut piece into a tube, and tape it. You will need one Gila Monster and one tube per child.

During the Program: Children glue pink and black beads on the Gila Monster, glue wiggle eyes on the Gila Monster, and glue the Gila Monster onto the paper tube. Then, they slide the paper tube over their fingers.

Read More About It

Bartlett, Richard. *Lizard Care from A to Z.* Barron's, 1997. Describes the care that is needed for lizards kept as pets.

Engfer, LeeAnne. *My Pet Lizards.* Lerner, 1999. Text and photos follow a boy as he explains how he takes care of his bearded dragon lizards and chameleons.

Martin, James. *Poisonous Lizards: Gila Monsters and Mexican Beaded Lizards.* Capstone Press, 1995. The habitat and physical characteristics of Gila Monsters and Mexican Beaded Lizards are discussed. Illustrated with photos.

Finger puppet pattern

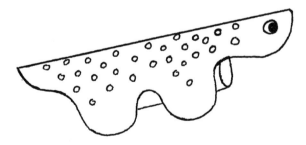

Sample finger puppet

Branded Books

In the days of the old west, it was necessary to mark cattle with a brand. Each ranch had its own brand. At round-up time, the cowboys could identify the cattle belonging to their ranch. Ranchers still brand their cattle to this day.

Description of Program

Each child constructs a brand book, designs a brand, and collects the brands of friends.

For ages: 7 and up

Length: 60 minutes

Limit: 30 children

Staff and volunteer requirements: One adult leader, a few adults to help with the sewing

Volunteer assignments: Cut the craft paper before the program. Assist the children with sewing the books during the program, to prevent injury from the needles.

Preparation time: 1 hour

Preparation: Purchase supplies. Gather books for display.

Craft: Branding Books

Supplies needed: One roll of brown craft paper, scissors, embroidery floss and needles with large eyes, markers and colored pencils, scrap paper for practicing drawing brands

Before the Program: Cut the craft paper into 4x8" sheets. You will need about five sheets per child.

During the Program: Allow the children to design their brand, using scrap paper. A few at a time, assist the children in constructing their brand books. Stack five sheets of brown paper. Fold them in half and unfold. Along the fold line, stitch the sheets together using embroidery floss. Be sure to tie a knot at the end of the floss before sewing, and another knot at the other end when the sewing is complete. It is very important to be careful with the needles, so no one gets stuck. When their brand books are constructed, children may draw their own brand on the first page. (See samples on p. 39.) They may ask their friends to draw their brands on the other pages, to complete their book.

Read More About It

Donati, Annabelle. *The Big Golden Book of the Wild West: American Indians, Cowboys and the Settling of the West.* Golden Books, 1991. The history of the West is shown with color illustrations and maps.

Herzig, Alison Cragin. *Bronco Busters.* Putnam, 1998. Three rough, tough, bronco busters can't tame a little black pony, but a small quiet cowboy does.

Pelta, Kathy. *Cattle Trails: Get Along Little Dogies.* Raintree Steck-Vaughn, 1997. Describes the history and customs of life along the American cattle trails.

Flying W

BB

Circle S

L and J

Mountain K

Bar C

Sample brands

Sponsor a Horse Service Project

Reading for a goal is a great motivator. If the goal is to assist with the care and feeding of a beautiful creature, many children will be excited to do it.

Description of Program

Contact one of agencies listed below, which maintain preserves for wild mustangs and American Indian horses. Cash donations are always needed for food, land, and veterinary care for the animals. Using funds solicited from a private source, your readers each make a donation to support wild horses, if the reading goal is met. The reading goal should be a challenge, but achievable. Keep a chart for the duration of your reading program, so children will know if they are getting close to the goal. You may obtain photos of the horses from the agency you are working with to help the children get to know the horses they are working to support. When the goal is achieved, celebrate by handing out horse pencils, a donation card, or a horse bookmark to each child who helped with the project.

Agencies Supporting Wild Horse Preservation

Wild Horse Preserves:
Bighorn Canyon National Recreation Area
Visitor Center
PO Box 487
Lovell, WY 82431
307-548-2251

Pacific Wild Horse Club
PO Box 1526
Eugene, OR 97440-1526

Wild Spirit Horse Preserve
1131 South 11th Street
Manitowoc, WI 54220
920-682-7863

Wild Horse/Burro Adoption:

The Bureau of Land Management has wild horses and burros which can be adopted for a fee, if certain requirements are met. If your reading group is in a rural area, and someone has space for such an animal, perhaps this is possible for you to do.

Bureau of Land Management
National Wild Horse and Burro Program
PO Box 12000
Reno, NV 89520-0006

Read More About It

Adams, Patricia and Jean Marxollo. *The Helping Hands Handbook: A Guide For Kids Who Want to Help People, Animals, and the World We Live In.* Random House, 1992. This book has over 100 projects kids can really do to help at home, in their community, with the environment, and around the world.

Ancona, George. *Man and Mustang.* Macmillan, 1992. This book describes the government program which maintains an ecological balance among wild mustangs by capturing, training, and offering for adoption selected animals.

Hobbs, Will. *The Big Wander.* Atheneum, 1992. As he searches for his uncle through the rugged Southwest canyon country, Clay becomes involved with a group of Navajo Indians who are trying to save some of the last wild mustangs.

Silverstein, Alvin. *The Mustang.* Millbrook Press, 1997. This book describes the habits and habitats of wild mustangs and some of the efforts being made to save these horses from extinction.

3 Diving for Treasure

What could be more fun than spending time at the sea? Let this theme take you there! Pirates, treasure maps, shells, sandy beaches, dolphins, and ancient tales of mermaids and Atlantis make Diving for Treasure a reading theme to be remembered. You may want to decorate your reading area with fishing nets and shells and display books in a treasure chest. Encourage your little pirates to loot your book shelves often! Here's how: hide bookmarks in shelved books, which children can trade in for a small prize, a fine-free day, or a ticket to a special event if they check out or read the book. Children will learn to treasure their own creativity at the craft programs, and will dive into the sea stories. A book donation service project gives children an opportunity to treasure others in their community.

Print a treasure map that serves as a place for reading goal selection and tracking. A sample treasure map is included on p. 42. Awards for this theme can be sea shells or gold-colored coins. You may solicit coupons from a swimming pool or a seafood restaurant. Perhaps a pet store will give a coupon for a free goldfish for each of your readers. A beach party could be given at the end of the theme for all children who reach their reading goal. Either hold the party at a swimming pool, or create the illusion of a beach on the grounds outside (or inside) your building.

Diving for Treasure
Reading Record

Select your reading goal from the treasures on this map.

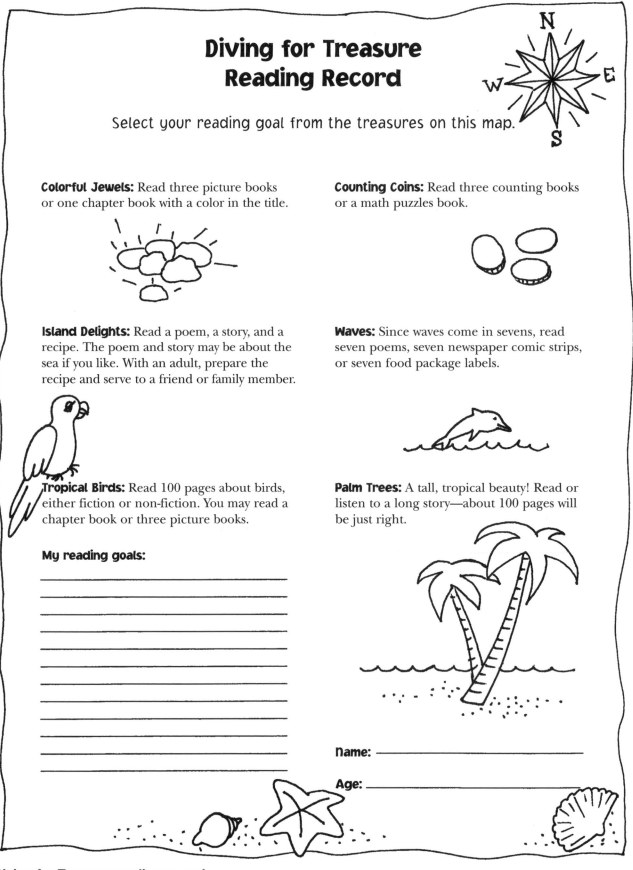

Colorful Jewels: Read three picture books or one chapter book with a color in the title.

Counting Coins: Read three counting books or a math puzzles book.

Island Delights: Read a poem, a story, and a recipe. The poem and story may be about the sea if you like. With an adult, prepare the recipe and serve to a friend or family member.

Waves: Since waves come in sevens, read seven poems, seven newspaper comic strips, or seven food package labels.

Tropical Birds: Read 100 pages about birds, either fiction or non-fiction. You may read a chapter book or three picture books.

Palm Trees: A tall, tropical beauty! Read or listen to a long story—about 100 pages will be just right.

My reading goals:

_____

_____

_____

_____

_____

_____

_____

_____

_____

_____

_____

Name: _____

Age: _____

Diving for Treasure reading record

Dolphin Drawings

Dolphins are beautiful and intelligent animals. Many children have a special fondness for them. This program provides children an opportunity to learn more about dolphins and practice drawing them.

Description of Program

Decorate the story area with dolphin posters, picture books, videos, and figures. Read a book about dolphins, then assist the children with the word search (see p. 44), asking questions and providing answers to reinforce the basic physical characteristics of dolphins. Then give the children drawing paper and pencils. Using the three-step drawing sheet as a guide (see p. 45), have the volunteer assist children in practicing their dolphin drawings. After several attempts have been made at drawing these dolphins, tell the children they may draw from the posters or books in the room.

For ages: 7 and up

Length: 60 minutes

Limit: 30 children

Staff or volunteer requirements: One adult reader and one volunteer

Volunteer assignments: The volunteer should be a skilled student or artist. They will assist the children with their drawings, demonstrate drawings, and give encouragement.

Preparation time: 1 hour

Preparation: Select book to be read, and collect display materials. Make enough copies of the word search for each child. Purchase or gather drawing paper and pencils.

Supplies needed: Dolphin poster(s), dolphin picture books, dolphin videos, rubber dolphin figures, copies of the word search, drawing paper, drawing pencils

Community resources needed: A skilled volunteer to instruct the drawing portion of the program

Read More About It

DuBosque, D.C. *Draw! Ocean Animals*. Peel Productions, 1994. Shows steps for drawing marine animals.

Elsebach, Angelika. *Sharks, Whales and Other Sea Creatures*. Dorling Kindersley Publishing, 1998. You Can Draw Series. Shows steps for drawing a variety of sea animals.

George, Twig C. *A Dolphin Named Bob*. HarperCollins, 1996. A very sick dolphin is nursed back to health by the staff of a marine aquarium and years later has a baby that becomes the star of the show there.

Orr, Katherine Shelly. *Story of A Dolphin*. Carolrhoda Books, 1993. Laura's father succeeds in befriending a dolphin, and helps the other people on the island learn to respect the dolphin's rights and feelings.

Provost, John F. *Common Dolphins*. Abdo and Daughters Publishers, 1995. Describes the physical characteristics and habits of the species of dolphins known as Common or Pacific.

Dolphin Word Search

Find and circle the words listed below.

r	e	p	p	i	l	f	s
b	l	o	w	h	o	l	e
s	m	o	o	t	h	u	k
o	c	e	a	n	a	k	s
m	a	m	m	a	l	e	a
a	l	e	a	p	o	s	s
c	f	i	n	f	a	s	t

blowhole   flukes

calf   mammal

fast   ocean

fin   sea

flipper   smooth

leap

How to Draw Dolphins

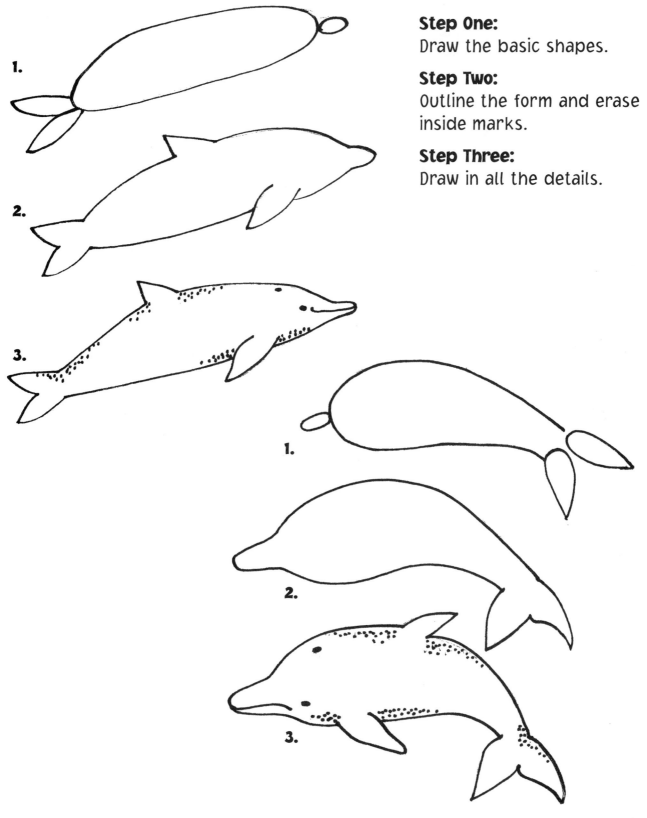

Step One:
Draw the basic shapes.

Step Two:
Outline the form and erase inside marks.

Step Three:
Draw in all the details.

Pirate Map

The excitement and adventure of pirates and map making are the focus of this program. Children will learn more about pirates from books, a game, and a map-following activity. They also create a pirate map of their own. Decorate accordingly with treasure chests and fish nets.

Description of Program

Invite the children to dress like a pirate for this program. Read a book about pirates to the children and discuss the use of a chest for buried treasure and a treasure map for locating the treasure later. Then, direct the children in the game, "Pirate's Trunk." Discuss the basics of map reading, and lead the children in following a map to a treasure that has been hidden in the building. Then, return the group to the program area, and have each child create a pirate map to take home. A coloring sheet may be given as a take-home project (see p. 47).

For ages: 5–9

Length: 45 minutes

Limit: 20 children

Staff or volunteer requirements: One adult

Preparation time: 2 hours

Preparation: Select pirate books to display and one to read. Purchase small treasures, such as pencils, bookmarks, or toys to hide in the building. Create a treasure map that leads to the treasure. Collect the materials for the craft. Decorate the library. Make copies of the coloring sheet for each child.

Supplies needed: Brown craft paper or brown grocery bags; markers, colored pencils, or crayons

Game: "Pirates Trunk"

Tell the children that they are going to pack a pirate's trunk with coins, jewels, pocket watches and many more things. The children make an alphabetical list of things going in the pirate's trunk, each child taking a turn. They may include items that would never go into a trunk—the funnier the better. The first child starts with the letter "A," saying, "I put an apple in the pirate's trunk." The second child adds to the list saying, "I put an apple and a baseball in the pirate's trunk." Each child adds to the list until someone cannot recall the list correctly. That child is out. The play continues until only one child remains.

Craft: Pirate Map

Each child is given a 9" x 12" sheet of brown craft paper or a piece of a brown paper bag. Using markers, crayons, or colored pencils the children create a treasure map. It is customary to mark the treasure spot with an "X". When they are finished, the children may tear the edges and crumple the paper to give it character.

Read More About It

Bramwell, Martyn. *How Maps are Made.* Lerner, 1998. Describes the history of mapmaking and provides instructions for making maps.

Kozar, Richard. *Infamous Pirates.* Chelsea House, 1999. Profiles 25 male and female sea robbers who stalked the oceans from the Spanish Main to the East Indies.

Rocklin, Joanne. *The Case of the Backyard Treasure.* Scholastic, 1998. Liz the Whiz and her younger brother use codes, a chart, and a map of the backyard to solve a mystery. Includes a section with related activities.

Stienecker, David. *Maps.* Benchmark Press, 1998. Points out the information found on maps and offers suggestions for further study.

Pirate coloring sheet

Lost City of Atlantis

Atlantis is a fascinating place. Teach children the legend of Atlantis, and provide them with an opportunity to experience group decision-making and cooperation through the creation of an Atlantis-like island.

Description of Program

Tell the children about the lost island City of Atlantis. Have the children create a model of the island together from sand in a wading pool. Then, give the children a passport to Atlantis as a souvenir of the program (see p. 49).

For ages: 5–9

Length: 30 minutes

Limit: 20 children

Staff requirements: One adult and one volunteer

Volunteer assignments: Assist at the program, giving out the digging tools and blocks. Help clean the children's hands after the program. Help clean up the area after the program.

Preparation time: 1 hour

Preparation: Prepare to talk or read about Atlantis to the group. Collect the necessary supplies. Make a copy of the passport for each child to take home.

Supplies needed: Small plastic wading pool; clean, damp sand; blocks, miniature people; sand digging tools such as shovels, spoons, and scoops; twigs and leaves for making trees

Storytime

To help the children understand what Atlantis was, you may read the following description of the place, and discuss with them whether it was a real place or a legend.

The Legend of the Lost City of Atlantis

Long ago, there was a special island called Atlantis. It was described by the Greek philosopher, Plato, as an island with a perfect climate, fertile soil, and peaceful, happy people. On this island there were ten kings and ten kingdoms. The kings agreed never to make war on each other. In the center of the island was the capital city, which was also called Atlantis, which was circular with a hill in the middle. On the hill was a temple where the ten kings met to discuss their kingdoms. Everything was wonderful on Atlantis. Everyone shared and did their part of the work, and had plenty of food and a good place to live. It seemed like nothing could ever change, because life on Atlantis was so perfect. Then one day, there was a huge earthquake that shook the island and caused a huge tidal wave. The whole island of Atlantis sunk beneath the sea. No one is sure if it was real. No one is even sure where Atlantis was. Plato thought Atlantis was in the Atlantic Ocean. Maybe some day we will find evidence beneath the ocean, and then we will know for sure where Atlantis was. Until then, we will just think of it as a story—a good story—about a perfect place where everyone got along well, and everyone was happy.

Read More About It

Ellis, Richard. *Imagining Atlantis.* Alfred A. Knopf, 1998. Relates the story in Plato's writings and follows theories of scientists, archaeologists, and science fiction writers about Atlantis.

Stein, Wendy. *Atlantis.* Greenhaven Press, 1998. This adult book discusses opposing viewpoints about the lost continent of Atlantis.

Sullivan, Robert. *Atlantis Rising: The True Story of a Submerged Land* Yesterday and Today. Simon & Schuster, 1999. An adult book about Atlantis, that separates historical truth from legends with rare documents and photographs.

Passport to Atlantis

This certificate allows the person named below to visit Atlantis anytime by wishing, dreaming, or imagining a place where everyone is happy.

_____

Name

Passport to Atlantis pattern

Starfish Art

The rhythm of the waves, the endless blue water, and the amazing creatures that live in the sea are a fascination. This program uses poetry and printmaking to explore the beauty of the sea.

Description of Program

Give each child a starfish nametag to wear at the program (see pattern on p. 51). Have children collaboratively compose a poem about the sea, and individually create a starfish print. First, read one or two books about sea animals, including starfish, showing photographs and discussing the similarities and differences between the animals. Then read several poems about underwater animals or the beach. The children write a poem as a group, with your guidance. Then the children create a starfish print.

For ages: 5–9

Length: 30 minutes

Limit: 30 children

Staff or volunteer requirements: One adult and one or two volunteers

Volunteer assignments: Someone who is experienced at writing poetry will assist the children in composing their poem. A young adult volunteer will cut out name tags before the program, assist with the printmaking portion of the program, and with cleaning up.

Preparation time: One hour

Preparation: Select books to read. Select a volunteer to help with the poetry writing, and one to help with the print making. Gather the print-making supplies.

Supplies needed: Newspapers for covering tables; apples, one for every two children; tempera paint; art paper for printing; foam plates for tempera paint; paint shirt or apron for each child (or instruct them to bring their own)

Poetry Writing Exercise

Select a subject for the poem: the beach, octopus, starfish. Gather descriptive words from the group about this subject, and write them on a board. Arrange the words into a poem, thinking of the visual effect and the sounds of the words.

This poem may be similar to the one your group will create.

The Sea by Kathryn Totten

Waves
    chasing my feet
      Sand squishing
    between my toes
Seagulls calling
    Come
      Find
    Little treasures
on the beach.

Craft: Starfish Prints

Cover work area with newspapers, and have each child wear a protective shirt or apron. Slice apples, revealing the star shape in the center made by the seeds. Pour tempera paint into foam plates. Allow the child to dip one half apple into the paint, then apply it to the art paper. A star pattern is created.

Read More About It

Butterfield, Moira. *Animals in the Oceans*. Raintree Steck-Vaughn, 1999. Introduces some of the animals that live in the oceans, including jellyfish, whales, manta rays, and starfish.

Florian, Douglas. *In the Swim: Poems and Paintings*. Harcourt Brace, 1997. A collection of humorous poems about underwater creatures.

Schwartz, David M. *Animal Eyes*. Gareth Stevens, 1999. Introduces in simple text and photographs the eyes of crabs, fish, frogs, and starfish.

Stefoff, Rebecca. *Starfish*. Benchmark Books, 1997. Text and photographs introduce more than 3000 kinds of starfish.

Starfish nametag pattern

Sand Painting

Sand has a wonderful texture. Children will explore various textures, listen to stories about the beach, and use the texture of sand to create a painting.

Description of Program

Decorate the story area with a beach umbrella, a beach ball, some shells, and a blanket. Play an ocean sounds recording softly in the background. Read a selection of books about the beach. Then, talk about textures, and pass around some objects with a variety of textures. The children then create a sand painting.

For ages: 5 and up

Length: 45 minutes

Limit: 30 children

Staff or volunteer requirements: One adult and one volunteer

Volunteer assignments: Assist the children with the sand painting and assist with clean-up after the program.

Preparation time: 1–2 hours

Preparation: Select the books to read. Purchase the art supplies. Gather items for decorating the room. Gather the items for the textures discussion.

Supplies needed: Newspapers for working area; colored craft sand; white, 9x12" posterboard for each child; cotton swabs; white glue; assorted small shells

Suggestions for textures discussion: Sand paper, velvet, feather, golf ball, pine cone, lemon, carpet

Craft: Sand Painting

Cover the working area with newspapers. The children draw a shape on the posterboard with the white glue, using a cotton swab to spread the glue around. The children sprinkle colored sand on the area. A second shape maybe drawn, and a second color applied. The children should be encouraged to draw their own design.

Read More About It

Daly, Niki. *The Boy on the Beach.* Margaret K. McElderry Books, 1999. Reluctant to let the surf crash over him, Joe runs down the beach and has an adventure with an old boat.

Garne, S. T. *One White Sail: A Caribbean Counting Book.* Green Tiger Press, 1992. A counting book in rhyme describing the sights found on an island beach.

Hayles, Marsha. *Beach Play.* Henry Holt, 1998. The sunny beach offers many fun and exciting activities for those who spend a day playing on its warm sands and in the water.

Lee, Huy Voun. *At the Beach.* Henry Holt, 1994. A mother amuses her young son at the beach by drawing Chinese characters in the sand.

A Day at the Ocean

The ocean has inspired many artists, authors, and song writers. Children will learn old jump rope rhymes about the ocean, listen to seaside books, and create a mini ocean to take home.

Description of Program

First, read a selection of books to introduce the ocean. Next, teach a jump rope rhyme, and have the children jump with it. If time permits, teach another rhyme, and give the children another chance to jump. During the last 10 minutes of the program, have the children create an ocean in a bag to take home.

For ages: 7 and up

Length: 30–45 minutes

Limit: 30 children

Staff or volunteer requirements: One adult and one volunteer

Volunteer assignments: Cut out the fish shapes from the craft foam, using the pattern included. Fill one plastic bag with blue hair gel for each participant. Hold one end of the jump rope, and assist with teaching the rhymes. Assist with the craft and with clean-up after the program.

Preparation time: 1–2 hours

Preparation: Select books to be read. Purchase craft materials. Learn the jump rope rhymes. Borrow or purchase a long jump rope.

Supplies needed: Blue hair gel; zip-closure, sandwich-size plastic bags; small shells; clear beads; craft foam; clear, plastic package sealing tape

Jump Rope Rhymes

A sailor went to sea, sea, sea
To see what he could see, see, see
And all that he could see, see, see
Was the bottom of the deep blue sea, sea, sea.

Drip drop, drip drop
down by the sea.
Up popped a mermaid,
she said to me:
"Skip in the middle,
one at each end.
Each is a sister,
each is a friend."

There are two holders for the jump rope. They turn it overhead, and a child jumps in. Everyone recites the rhyme while the child jumps. If she misses, meaning she steps on the rope or fails to jump in time, another jumper enters the rope, and everyone starts the rhyme where they left off. Continue until everyone gets a chance to jump at least once. Substitute a new rhyme if desired. Continue jumping for about 15 minutes.

Craft: Ocean in a Bag

Distribute a zip-closure, sandwich-size plastic bag which has been pre-filled with blue hair gel to a thickness of ¼". Each child places a few sea shells, a few plastic beads for bubbles, and a few tiny fish cut from colored craft foam (see patterns on p. 54). Seal the bag well with the zipper top. Slide the bag into another plastic bag and seal that bag also, squeezing out any extra air. Seal the top of this bag with clear tape. This mini ocean is very soothing to squeeze, and the fish and shells will move around, appearing to swim in the water.

Read More About It

Berenstain, Stan. *The Berenstain Bears by the Sea.* Random House, 1998. Before the Bear family can swim in the ocean there is a lot of work to be done.

Farber, Norma. *I Swim an Ocean in My Sleep.* Henry Holt, 1997. A dream takes the reader into the ocean world with its coral castle and dancing lobsters.

Ray, Mary Lyn. *Alvah and Arvilla.* Harcourt Brace, 1994. Arvilla has never been able to see the ocean, but she gets an idea that will allow her and the whole farm to travel to the Pacific.

Tiny fish patterns for "Ocean in a Bag"

Shell Creatures

Shells come in a variety of shapes and colors. Children will become acquainted with some of the animals that live in shells. And, with some imagination, and a little glue, shells can be turned into fantasy creatures.

Description of Program

Give children a shell nametag to wear at the program (see patterns on p. 56). First, show photographs of shelled animals, and briefly discuss what kinds of animals live in shells. Then, have the children play a game called "Clam Shell." After the game, help the children create a shell creature using a variety of shells, wiggle eyes, and pipe cleaners. They may create something that resembles an animal or create a totally new creature.

For ages: 5 and up

Length: 30–45 minutes

Limit: 30 children

Staff or volunteer requirements: One adult and one volunteer

Volunteer assignments: Cut out name tags. Assist the children with the craft and assist with clean-up after the program.

Preparation time: 1 hour

Preparation: Select books to be read. Purchase craft supplies.

Supplies needed: Shells in assorted sizes, about five per child; wiggle eyes, two per child; beads in a variety of colors and shapes; pipe cleaners; scissors; tacky craft glue

Game: "Clam Shell"

First, write a list on a board including a variety of sea creatures such as starfish, dolphin, seahorse, whale, oyster, shark—clam.

Discuss which of these animals have shells. Tell them the object of the game is to find a clam shell. Seat the children on the floor in a circle. Select one person to be "It." This person walks outside the circle touching the heads of each child saying the name of any sea creature except "Clam." Finally, "It" touches one child and says "Clam." That child chases "It" around the outside of the circle, trying to tag him before he gets back to the open space and sits down. If tagged, "It" continues. If he makes it back to the open space before being tagged, the standing child is the new "It". The game continues for about 10 minutes.

Craft: Shell Creatures

Each child selects four or five small shells. Using craft glue, the child puts them together to form a creature. It may resemble a real animal, or it may be something from their imagination. The child may cut pieces of pipe cleaner to create feelers or arms, and he may glue wiggle eyes on his creature.

Read More About It

Abbott, R. Tucker. *Seashells of the World: A Guide to the Better-known Species*. Golden Press, 1991. Photographs of many shells.

Fowler, Allan. *Shellfish Aren't Fish*. Children's Press, 1998. Provides information about oysters, clams, scallops, and mussels.

Patchett, Lynne. *My Shell*. Gareth Stevens, 1995. Shells come in many colors shapes, sizes, and patterns. The reader must try to find a particular shell that is big and has stripes.

Dance, S. Peter. *Eyewitness Handbooks: Shells*. Dorling Kindersley, 1991. Describes the behavior, anatomy, and inner workings of various shelled animals.

Shell nametag patterns

Book Treasures Service Project

Children who love to read will be excited to participate in this project. Books are treasures that can be shared with others, and sharing gives children a feeling of importance and generosity.

Description of Program

Think of some places in your community where children must wait. This could be doctors' or dentists' offices, the motor vehicle office, or shelters for homeless families. Contact some of these places, and get permission to place Book Treasure Bags in their facility.

There are two ways to create the cloth bags. The first is a printing project. The second is a sewing project. Choose the method that best suits your community, your resources, and your volunteers.

The children donate used paperback books in good condition, and sort them by age and interest level. If desired, they may rubber stamp the inside of the books or place bookplates in them to indicate that they were donated for the Book Treasures Project. The children will feel good about recycling books they have already read, and they will enjoy stamping the books and choosing

three or four for a bag. Then, distribute these treasure bags to the selected facilities.

You may want to celebrate by handing out a certificate or bookmark to each child who donates books or helps with the sorting and stamping.

Craft: Book Treasures Book Bags

Option One, Painted Bags: Purchase blank canvas bags and fabric paint. Allow children to use stencils (see samples on p. 58) or potato prints of fish, shells, sea horses, or whales to decorate the bags. You must have one bag per child.

Option Two, Sewn Bags: Sew cloth bags from fabric with a sea creatures print (see patterns on p. 57). You will need adult volunteers to sew the bags. The children will participate by selecting and placing the books in the bags. Any number may participate.

Bookmark design

Sea creature print designs

Turn Back the Pages of Time

Traveling to distant lands can be so much fun! The Turn Back the Pages of Time reading theme will take you far away, and far back in time as well. Children will participate in the Olympics in Ancient Greece, learn to rope a horse in the Wild West, and maybe become a mummy in Ancient Egypt. Decorations for this theme can include pictures of castles, pyramids, or Viking ships. Encourage your readers to be Renaissance men and women by reading about art, music, and science. They will try their hand at ancient art forms such as pottery making and quilt making.

The reading choices are like a feast fit for a Queen or a Pharaoh, and the sample reading record reflects that idea (see p. 60). Awards can be tiny toy cowboys, rings with beautiful jewels, or Olympic medals. At the end of this theme, you may hold a royal picnic on the grounds outside your building (or indoors) with musical entertainment.

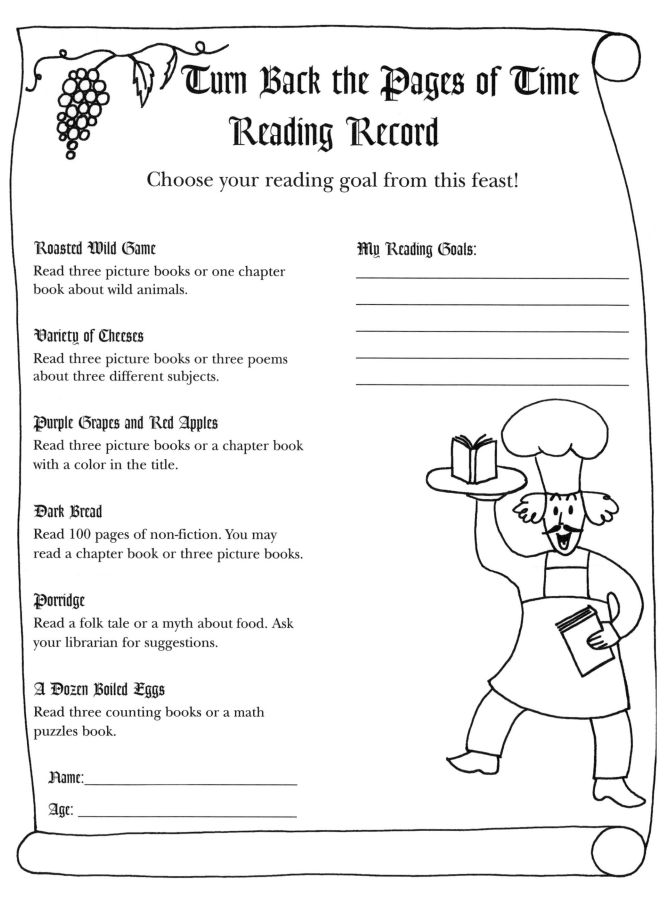

Turn Back the Pages of Time
Reading Record

Choose your reading goal from this feast!

Roasted Wild Game

Read three picture books or one chapter book about wild animals.

Variety of Cheeses

Read three picture books or three poems about three different subjects.

Purple Grapes and Red Apples

Read three picture books or a chapter book with a color in the title.

Dark Bread

Read 100 pages of non-fiction. You may read a chapter book or three picture books.

Porridge

Read a folk tale or a myth about food. Ask your librarian for suggestions.

A Dozen Boiled Eggs

Read three counting books or a math puzzles book.

My Reading Goals:

_____

_____

_____

_____

Name:_____

Age: _____

Voyage with the Vikings

The Vikings were great sailors and great warriors. This program introduces children to the Viking way of life through games, crafts, and activities.

Description of Program

Begin the program with a game where children learn about the Viking class system. Then, have them make Thor's hammer pendants (see pattern on p. 62). While the pendants are being spray painted, teach them more about Viking culture and have them complete a word search (see p. 63). The final activity is stringing the pendants for necklaces to wear home.

For ages: 6 and up

Length: 45 minutes

Limit: 30 children

Staff or volunteer requirements: One adult and one or two young adult volunteers

Volunteer assignment: Trace the pattern on corrugated cardboard and cut out one for each child. Punch a hole near the top, as shown on the pattern, for the string. Cut a 30" piece of string for each child. Make copies of the word search for each child. Make signs for the game. During the game, help determine the winning team. Take the hammers outside, and in a newspaper-covered area, spray paint them.

Preparation time: 2 hours

Preparation: Be sure signs, word search, and hammers are prepared. Buy string and spray paint. Prepare to lead the game and word search activity. Purchase small prizes for the winners of the Viking People game.

Supplies needed: Corrugated cardboard, string, silver spray paint, dull-pointed pencils

Sample facts to share about the Vikings:

Vikings lived in Norway and Denmark. They also settled in Sweden and Iceland. They were good ship builders, and sailed to other countries in Europe. Sometimes they raided or robbed people on these voyages. Sometimes they went as honest traders.

The Vikings lived on farms where they raised goats and cattle for milk. They ate many dairy foods, such as milk, buttermilk, and cheese. Also, they grew grains for making bread. They caught fish in the sea and in the rivers. They preserved their meat and fish by drying or salting. Many times, they cooked their meat over an open fire. Other times, they boiled their meat in a cauldron, or pot, hung over the fire.

The Vikings made their houses out of blocks of grass or turf, because wood was not plentiful. Their houses were rectangular with a fire pit in the middle. They were called "long houses."

The Vikings liked to fight, and they made great swords. They wanted to go to Heaven, which was reserved for men who died fighting. Viking heaven was called "Valhalla."

Game: "Viking People"

As the children come into the story area, a sign is pinned to their back saying "Jarl," "Karl," or "Thrall." On the wall are three large signs with the same three words on them. The children are seated on the floor while you explain the game as follows:

In the days of the Vikings, people were divided into three social classes. The Jarls were the wealthy land owners. They were powerful and respected by the others. The Karls were also fairly rich. They owned their own farms, or worked on the farms of their friends or relatives. The Thralls were slaves. They worked hard, and were given food and shelter, but they were not free to come and go as they pleased. They had to do whatever the Jarls or Karls told them to do. If the Thralls worked hard enough, they could earn their freedom and become a Karl.

You have a sign on your back. Written on the sign is "Jarl," "Karl," or "Thrall." You must ask questions to find out who you are. When you have guessed, sit on the floor by the correct sign on the wall. The first group to get all their members wins, and every member gets a prize.

Questions:

1. Am I rich?

2. Am I a slave?

3. Do I own land?

4. Do I work for my friend?

5. Am I powerful?

The leader watches carefully to determine which group is first. You may ask a volunteer to help with this. The prize can be a toy ring or coin.

Craft: Thor's Hammer Necklace

The children are seated at tables. The leader explains that Thor was one of the Viking gods. Vikings made silver jewelry in the shape of Thor's hammer, which was worn for good luck.

Each child is given a cardboard cut-out of Thor's hammer. Using a dull pencil, a design is embossed on the hammer by pushing the pencil tip through the first layer of cardboard, making the small holes. (See the pattern below.) After the children have embossed their hammer, they write their name on the back. A volunteer collects the hammers, takes them to an outside area covered with newspapers, and spray paints them silver. Then, the children thread a string through the hole, and tie it to complete the necklace.

Read More About It

James, John. *How we Know About the Vikings*. P. Bed rick, 1997. An illustrated account of the customs and everyday life of the Vikings.

Martell, Hazel. *Food and Feasts with the Vikings*. New Discovery Books, 1995. Discusses the social life and food of Scandinavia and the ancient Vikings.

Speed, Peter. *Harald Hardrada and the Vikings*. Raintree/Steck-Vaughn, 1993. Describes the origins, activities, and invasions of the Vikings.

Wright, Rachel. *Vikings: Facts, Things to Make, Activities*. F. Watts, 1992. Describes the Viking way of life and provides instructions for related craft projects.

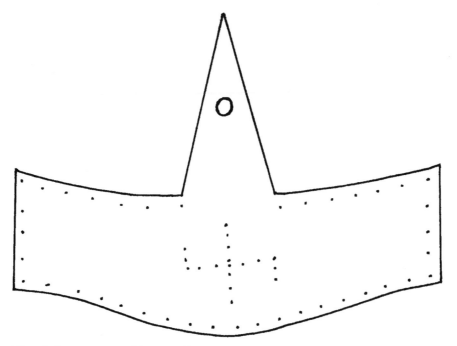

Thor's hammer necklace pattern

Viking Word Search

Find and circle the words listed below.
They may read up, down, diagonal or across

```
F D N I S Q I V S N N M W H M
D N K A G A A G K T Q E P D E
P L I L M L N B L R A J V R X
S L R Z H I O T A Q A T T A Q
R S R A K W R A I T Q M U I B
E E L I K I W C E B H H N D V
D L V N P I A Z O K M A A E J
A X C Z F B Y F Y K J X P P D
R C N O R D L U A C M B E I Z
T W H E O A W T H R A L L H O
V H A E A L I T U R F K U S W
D D C H E A E S S N F G M P Y
K F S F C S C S Z W S M A B N
J I Y V T Y E I N M Y K O Y W
F U A X C V A V Y W P G E V X
```

1. bath
2. bread
3. cauldron
4. cheese
5. Denmark
6. fish
7. Jarl
8. Karl
9. Norway
10. raid
11. sail
12. sea
13. ship
14. thrall
15. traders
16. turf
17. Valhalla
18. Vikings

A Visit to Ancient Rome

The Roman Empire was rich with stories. This program introduces children to the Roman Empire and its mythology, and includes a take-along craft.

Description of Program

Give the children an Ancient Rome nametag to wear (see pattern on p. 66). Provide background information about the Roman Empire, showing where it was on a world map. Then, share the story of Damon and Pythias from Roman mythology on the p. 65. Finally, help the children make a Damon and Pythias friendship pin to take home.

Some facts to share about the Roman Empire:

- The Roman Empire began about 800 years BC as a small village in western Italy. By 250 AD, the city of Rome had grown to more than 1 million people, and included lands in Europe and Africa.

- In 79 AD, a volcano known as Vesuvius erupted, covering the Roman city of Pompeii. Many clues about how the Romans lived and what they ate were buried under the lava.

- Pasta, bread, spicy sausage, and olives were common foods in Italy. Olives were often pressed into oil, and spices and herbs were used to flavor food. Romans also liked to hunt and eat wild deer and boar. Some domestic animals were raised, including cows, sheep, pigs, and goats.

- The language of Ancient Rome was Latin, and many languages spoken in Europe today came from Latin.

- Roman mythology includes many gods. Many of the stories come from Greek mythology, but the names of the gods have been changed.

For ages: 5–12

Length: 30 minutes

Limit: 30 children

Staff or volunteer requirements: One adult leader, optional volunteer

Volunteer assignments: Assist with the friendship pin activity.

Preparation time: 1 hour

Preparation: Prepare to discuss Ancient Rome and tell the myth. Purchase supplies for the friendship pins.

Supplies needed: Seed beads in a variety of colors and safety pins

Craft: Damon and Pythias Friendship Pins

Instruct the children to select a variety of beads and slide them onto an open safety pin. Fasten the pin to a shoelace or shirt collar. Tell the children that if they make two alike, they can give one to their best friend to wear.

Read More About It

Chalk, Gary. *Gary Chalk's Hide and Seek in History.* Dorling Kindersley, 1997. Join the Scavengers as they travel in their time machine to different periods and places including Ancient Rome.

Hinds, Kathryn. *The Ancient Romans.* Benchmark Books, 1997. Explores the culture of Ancient Rome.

Hoffman, Mary. *A First Book of Myths: Myths and Legends for the Very Young from Around the World.* Dorling Kindersley, 1999. Greek, Roman, Australian, Norse, and other myths are retold.

Mann, Elizabeth. *The Roman Colosseum.* Mikaya Press, 1998. Describes the building of the Colosseum in ancient Rome and tells how it was used.

Pickels, Dwayne. *Roman Myths, Heroes and Legends.* Chelsea House, 1999. Presents biographical sketches of 25 gods and goddesses of Roman mythology from Apollo to Vesta.

The Story of Damon and Pythias

Long ago in Ancient Rome, two young noble men were best friends. Their names were Damon and Pythias.

The ruler of their city was a cruel man named Dionysius. For no reason at all, Dionysius put Pythias in prison and sentenced him to die. Pythias could not prove that he was innocent, no matter how he tried. Pythius asked Dionysius for a favor.

"Let me go home to say good-bye to my family before I die," he asked.

Dionysius said, "Sure, you may go, if you can get someone to take your place in prison. If you don't come back in time, that person will die in your place." Dionysius laughed. He was sure no one would agree to that.

Pythias asked his best friend, Damon, to take his place. Damon agreed immediately. He was not afraid. He trusted Pythias to come back in time, so he would not have to die in his place.

Pythias went home to see his family.

Finally the day came, and Pythias still had not returned. Dionysius commanded that Damon would have to die in place of his friend. Damon was calm. He smiled and said, "My friend will come in time, or I will die for him. It does not matter to me, because he is my friend."

The crowd sobbed in the courtyard. Damon was brought out in chains. Dionysius looked on with a sneer.

A runner was seen on the road, hurrying to the courtyard. It was Pythias. He ran to his friend and hugged him. The people cheered.

Dionysius could not believe it. He gave Pythias a pardon, and begged Damon and Pythias to be his friends. He said, "I have never had a true friend. You have taught me what it means to be a friend."

Ancient Rome nametag patterns

The Olympics of Ancient Greece

Ancient Greece was the site of the first Olympic games in 776 BC. Children learn about Ancient Greece through storytime and Olympic-style games.

Description of Program

Introduce the Olympic program by describing the Ancient Greek Olympic games. Invite children to participate in a number of athletic games. Create a display of books about Ancient Greece, and encourage children to check them out. The program can be held out on the lawn, or in a large room cleared of furniture.

Some facts to share about the Ancient Greek Olympic Games:

- Almost 1200 years ago, athletes came from all over Greece to take part in the Olympic Games in honor of the god Zeus.

- Athletes stayed in Olympia for several weeks to train for the games, and food and shelter was provided.

- At the beginning of the Olympics a torch was lit, marking the official opening of the games.

- The athlete who won the Olympic games was crowned with an olive wreath and was honored in his home city for life.

For ages: 3 and up

Length: 30–60 minutes

Limit: Any number of children may participate

Staff or volunteer requirements: Two adults

Volunteer assignments: Volunteers may make the paper torch and olive wreaths or ribbons for awards.

Preparation time: 1–2 hours

Preparation: Plan the races and games that are appropriate for your children. Collect the balls, bean bags, and other equipment that will be needed.

Game: Mini-Olympics

An older child is given a paper torch (see pattern on p. 68). He or she carries it around the room, or around the lawn area where your games will take place, while everyone else looks on with great respect. They place the torch in front, near the judges. Then, the games begin.

A number of games should be planned, such as a long jump, a relay race, a bean bag toss, and a short dash race. A ribbon or wreath can be given to the winner of each game.

Read More About It

Freeman, Charles. *The Ancient Greeks.* Oxford University Press, 1996. Various aspects of life in ancient Greece are described, including religion, government, the Olympics, and family life.

Hodges, Susie. *Ancient Greek Art.* Heinemann Interactive Library, 1998. Mosaics, pottery, sculpture, architecture, and painting of ancient Greece are discussed.

Granfield, Linda. *Circus: An Album.* Dorling Kindersley, 1998. A nonfiction adventure that traces the evolution of the circus, beginning with Ancient Egypt.

MacDonald, Fiona. *First Facts About the Ancient Greeks.* Peter Bedrick Books, 1997. Surveys food, hair styles, jewelry, and festivals.

Selberg, Jackie. *500 Five Minute Games: Quick and Easy Activities for 3 to 6 Year Olds.* Gryphon House, 1995. Easy games for small children are explained.

Olympic torch pattern

A Visit to Camelot

There is an air of mystery about King Arthur and Camelot. This program introduces the children to the legends of the Knights of the Round Table.

Description of Program

Introduce the legend of King Arthur and Camelot (see p. 70). After the introduction, have the children play a game called, "Journey to Camelot." Then give the children a coloring sheet to take home (see p. 71).

For ages: 5 and up

Length: 30 minutes

Limit: Any number of children may participate

Staff and volunteer requirements: One adult

Preparation time: 1 hour

Preparation: Prepare to tell the story of Arthur. Make copies of the coloring sheet. Select books to display.

Game: "Journey to Camelot"

Have children count off by fours, and divide them into four groups. Read a scenario, and direct each group to work together to make up an ending for the scenario. Give them five minutes to plan it. Then, have one person from each group tell that group's ending. Repeat with another scenario, if time permits.

Scenario #1: You are Sir Lancelot, the best friend of King Arthur. You have been away from Camelot, protecting small villages from robbers. Now you are on your way home. You stop for the night and make camp. You are happy, because tomorrow you will be home, and you will see your friend the king. You are almost asleep, when you hear a lady calling for help. What do you do?

Scenario #2: You are a traveling tinker. You repair pots and pans that have holes in them, or sharpen kitchen knives. You are in a village near the great city of Camelot. You have a lot of work to do in this village. Every evening, one of the families invites you to their cottage for supper. This night, as you eat a delicious stew with dark bread and honey, they tell you about something that has been scaring everyone in the village for a week. What is scaring them? Can you help them?

Scenario #3: You are a knight on your horse. On a bridge over a deep river, you meet another knight on his horse. The bridge is narrow, and he cannot pass you. You do not want to back up, and neither does he. He gives you a riddle. If you can guess it, he will let you pass. If not, he will knock you into the river. This is the riddle: I run, but I have no feet. I can carry you, but you cannot carry me. I have two banks, but no money. Can you guess the riddle? Do you get to go across the bridge, or will the other knight knock you into the river? (The answer to the riddle is: The River.)

Read More About It

Bulloch, Ivan. *I Wish I Were....A Princess.* World Book/Two-Can, 1996. Provides instructions for making costumes and handicrafts for a Princess and a Knight.

Carlson, Laurie. *Days of Knights and Damsels: An Activity Guide.* Chicago Review Press, 1998. More than 100 illustrated crafts and games help create the culture of the Middle Ages.

Kerven, Rosalind. *King Arthur.* Dorling Kindersley, 1998. A retelling of the story of the boy who became King of Camelot.

Maynard, Christoper. *Days of the Knights: A Tale of Castles and Battles.* Dorling Kindersley, 1998. Presents a day in the life of a medieval lord as he runs the land.

Sabuda, Robert. *Arthur and the Sword.* Atheneum, 1995. A retelling of Sir Malory's tale of young Arthur who proves to be the rightful heir to the throne by pulling a sword from a steel anvil.

Williams, Marcia. *King Arthur and the Knights of the Round Table.* Candlewick Press, 1996. Based on Sir Malory's story, this book retells the legend of King Arthur.

The Legend of King Arthur and Camelot

A long time ago, during the Middle Ages in England, there was a boy named Arthur. He was living with a foster family. He was much smaller than the other boys in the family, and it was his job to help them.

One time the whole family went to a tournament. This is where the men who wanted to be knights would practice fighting. They practiced sword fights and jousting while riding on horses. Arthur's foster brother, Sir Kay, was a strong young man. He wanted to be a knight. Arthur was proud of him. He thought Sir Kay would be a very good knight. Arthur helped him get dressed in his armor. Then Arthur looked around for Sir Kay's sword. He could not find it. He ran back to the inn where they stayed the night before to get the sword. He could not get in. Arthur really wanted to help Sir Kay. Without a sword, Sir Kay would not be allowed to compete in the tournament. Arthur saw a sword stuck in an iron anvil in the middle of a public square. No one was around. Arthur decided to try to get that sword for Sir Kay. He pulled on the handle, and he pulled the sword out. He ran to Sir Kay. Everyone saw the sword he was carrying. They all got very excited, because they knew it was the sword from the anvil. The people all bowed down to Arthur, even Sir Kay. He was confused! He was just a boy helping his brother. Then they explained that whoever could pull the sword from the iron anvil was the rightful King of England.

Arthur grew up and was a great King. He lived in a beautiful city called Camelot. He organized his knights and gave them a round table for their meetings so everyone would be equal. He encouraged his knights to fight for the good and protect their country. There are many stories about King Arthur and the Knights of the Round Table.

Knight coloring sheet

A Visit to Ancient Egypt

Egypt was a great civilization. This program introduces children to the culture that thrived in the valley of the Nile River.

Description of Program

Give children an Egyptian mask nametag to wear at the program (see p. 73). Share the following facts about Ancient Egypt or develop your own. Then, play the game, "Mummy Wrap," and end the program by making clay bowls.

Some facts to share about Ancient Egypt:

- Egypt was a great civilization that began almost 5000 years ago in 3,000 BC in northern Africa. Their rulers were called Pharaohs. The Pharaohs directed the building of the great Pyramids and the great Sphinx which remain today.

- People in Egypt wore simple clothes because the climate was hot all the time. Men and women wore a lot of jewelry. The Egyptians were great artists. They painted on the walls of the tombs. They were good at weaving linen. They made a form of paper for writing called "papyrus." They made beautiful pottery from clay found near the Nile River.

- When rich people died in Ancient Egypt, they were embalmed and wrapped with linen bandages. A body prepared this way is called a "mummy." Then they were buried with a gold death mask in an elaborate coffin. The tombs of the Pharaohs were in the great Pyramids.

For ages: 5 and up

Length: 30–45 minutes

Limit: 30 children

Staff and volunteer requirements: One adult and one volunteer

Volunteer assignments: Assist the children with the pottery project and with clean-up.

Preparation time: 1 hour

Preparation: Prepare to tell about ancient Egypt. Select books for display. Purchase materials.

Game: "Mummy Wrap"

Divide the children into two teams. Have each team select one person to be the "mummy." They wrap him or her with white crepe paper streamers, trying to cover them completely, starting from the feet and working up to the face. When the team has completely wrapped their mummy, the whole team sits down, leaving the mummy standing. The winning team members are declared the Pharaohs for the day.

Game supplies: Several rolls of white crepe paper streamers for each team.

Craft: Clay Bowls

Seat the children around tables covered with newspaper, and give each child a portion of self-hardening clay to work with. Show them how to construct a bowl in much the same way the ancient Egyptians made them:

Begin by forming a small, flat circle of clay, about 4" in diameter. Score the surface with a pencil along the outer edge, so the coils will stick. Roll a coil about ⅛" in diameter, and about 10 or 12" in length. Coil this around the base. Add more coils, building the bowl up. Once in awhile, score the edge before adding another coil, to be sure the coils will stick. When the bowl is about 4" tall, smooth the coils by hand. Make a neat edge on the top. Let the bowl dry in the air.

Craft supplies: Newspapers to cover work surface, self-hardening clay, pencils, paper towels for clean-up.

Read More About It

Bunting, Eve. *I Am the Mummy Heb-Nefert*. Harcourt Brace & Co. 1997. A mummy recalls her past life in ancient Egypt as the wife of the Pharaoh's brother.

Harvey, Miles. *Look What Came from Egypt*. Watts, 1998. Describes many familiar inventions, foods, customs, tools, toys, and fashions that originated in Ancient Egypt.

Haslam, Andrew. *Ancient Egypt*. Thomas Learning, 1995. Egyptian civilization is explored in a hands-on approach.

Hodges, Susie. *Ancient Egyptian Art*. Heinmann Interactive Library, 1998. Examines the art of ancient Egypt including wall paintings, reliefs, buildings, and sculpture.

King, David C. *Egypt: Ancient Traditions, Modern Hopes*. Benchmark Books, 1997. Discusses the geography, history, culture, daily life, and people of Egypt.

Egyptian mask nametag pattern

Return to the Renaissance

The Renaissance began in Italy in the 14th century, and in the rest of Europe in the 15th century. It was a time of great learning. This program introduces children to this era of great art, literature, and science.

Description of Program

Explain that during the Renaissance, there was an explosion of development and personal expression through art, music, literature, and science. Show samples of the art of Leonardo da Vinci, Michelangelo, Raphael, Albrecht Durer, or other Renaissance artists. Discuss the realistic style and subtle colors. Then, show a short video clip from a Shakespearean play, and a short clip from the "Man of La Mancha." Talk about how exciting it is to be able to read, show a diagram of the solar system, and give each child a Renaissance notebook.

Some facts to share about the Renaissance:

During the Renaissance, it became important to people that they learn to read and write. They learned a great deal about science and nature as well. There were many discussions about how the universe is organized, about the systems of the human body, and the laws of nature.

For ages: 7 and up

Length: 45 minutes

Limit: 30 children

Staff and volunteer requirements: One adult and one volunteer

Volunteer assignments: Make copies of the Renaissance notebook pages. Cut apart and staple the pages to make a notebook for each child.

Preparation time: 2–3 hours

Preparation: Collect art books to show. Find a video of a Shakespearean play and "The Man of La Mancha," and select a short clip to show. Collect science books and a diagram of the solar system to show.

Activity: My Renaissance Notebook

Have the children make their own Renaissance notebook (see patterns on p. 75-76). Explain that the notebooks are for them to record their favorite artists, thoughts about books, and ideas about science. Perhaps they can revisit them periodically and add new entries.

Read More About It

Daly, Niki. Bravo, *Zan Angelo!: A Commedia Dell'arte Tale with Story and Pictures.* Farrar Straus & Giroux, 1998. In Renaissance Venice, Angleo, wishing to be a famous clown as his grandfather, decides to do something special during the Carnival.

Howarth, Sarah. *Renaissance People.* Millbrook Press, 1992. Presents 13 vocations including banker, artist, and explorer.

Morrison, Taylor. *Antonio's Apprenticeship: Painting a Fresco in Renaissance Italy.* Holiday House, 1996. As an apprentice in his uncle's studio, Antonio learns that creating beautiful frescoes for a Florentine chapel takes patience.

Nesbitt, E. *The Best of Shakespeare.* Oxford University Press, 1997. Simplified prose retellings of Romeo and Juliet, Hamlet, and other plays.

Pinguilly, Yves. *Da Vinci: The Painter Who Spoke with Birds.* Chelsea House, 1994. A biography of the famous Renaissance artist.

My Renaissance Notebook

Name: _____

Artists I like:

Paintings I like:

Plays I like:

Renaissance notebook patterns

Books I like:

My ideas about science:

Music I like:

My ideas about math:

Renaissance notebook patterns

The Wild West

When America was a young country, people began to move from the East to the open spaces in the West. This was a wild place. It was important to know how to ride a horse, shoot a gun, and rope cattle. This program introduces children to the Wild West.

Description of Program

Encourage children to dress "western-style" for the program, and give them a nametag to wear that day (see pattern below). Read a selection of stories about the Wild West. If possible, a rancher or someone with a riding stable can show a saddle, bridle, and other tack. They can also show the children how to throw a lasso, and give the children a chance to try to toss the rope over a chair.

For ages: 5 and up

Length: 30–45 minutes

Limit: Any number of children may participate

Staff and volunteer requirements: One adult

Preparation time: 1 hour

Preparation: Select stories to read. Invite someone to show a saddle and other tack. Ask the person to demonstrate how to throw a lasso.

Community resources needed: Someone who works with horses to show a saddle and demonstrate how to throw a lasso.

Read More About It

Antle, Nancy. *Sam's Wild West Show.* Dial Books for Young Readers, 1995. Sam and his Wild West show entertain the townsfolk and catch two bank robbers.

Everett, Percival. *The One the Got Away.* Clarion Books, 1992. Three cowhands chase and corral ones in this zany book about the Wild West.

Saller, Carol. *Pug, Slug and Doug the Thug.* Carolrhoda Books, 1994. A humorous Wild West tale about a dog, a cat, and a boy who outwit the bad guys.

Spinner, Stephanie. *Little Sure Shot: The Story of Annie Oakley.* Random House, 1993. A biography of a poor farm girl who became the star of Buffalo Bill's Wild West Show.

Wood, Tim. *The Wild West.* Viking, 1998. The story of the American West is revealed in scenes of a cattle ranch, miners panning for gold, a frontier town, and a train.

Cowboy hat nametag pattern

Quilts for a Queen Service Project

Children will enjoy learning an ageless skill and feel the rewards of helping to create useful and beautiful quilts in this project.

Description of Program

With the assistance of quilters from your community, the children tie one or more baby quilts, which are then donated to a hospital or service agency in your area.

Preparation required: Contact a quilting club in your area and ask for a few volunteers to teach children how to tie a quilt. Ask for the quilters to provide the quilt frames.

For ages: 6 and up

Length: A baby quilt can be tied in about an hour, allowing for instruction time.

Limit: Any number of children may participate; plan on one quilt for every 10 children

Staff and volunteer requirements: One adult and a group of quilter volunteers.

Volunteer assignments: One volunteer can assist about 10 children in tying a quilt. Other volunteers will also be needed to finish the quilt edges after they are tied.

Preparation time: 2–3 hours

Preparation: Purchase supplies. Arrange for volunteers to assist the children with quilting and to finish the quilt edges. On the day of your quilt project, set up the quilt frames.

Supplies needed: Top fabric, quilt batting, and bottom fabric for each quilt you will make; quilt frames; yarn; thimbles; and large eye needles for tying the quilts

Craft: Quilt Making

Allow each child to make a few stitches, then have another child take a turn. You may want to have more than one quilt frame set up at a time, if your group is large enough.

The quilters may be willing to display a few of their quilts on the day of your program. This will allow the children to see a variety of quilt styles and patterns. They may see pieced quilts, applique quilts, tied quilts, and traditional quilts.

Note: Please do not let the children touch the display quilts, as dirt and oils on their hands can damage them.

Read More About It

Eikmeier, Barbara J. *Kids Can Quilt.* That Patchwork Place, 1997. Provides simple patchwork projects for machine quilting that children can do.

Hesse, Karen. *Lavender.* Holt, 1993. Codie's favorite aunt is having a baby, and she hopes her baby quilt will be finished on time.

Kinsey-Warnock, Natalie. *The Canada Geese Quilt.* Cobblehill Books, 1989. Ariel uses her artistic talent and her grandmother's knowledge to create a very special quilt for the coming new baby.

Paul, Ann Whitford. *Eight Hands Round: A Patchwork Alphabet.* HarperCollins, 1991. Introduces the letters of the alphabet with the names of early American patchwork quilt patterns.

5 Books and All That Jazz

This is a reading theme to get everyone all jazzed up! Explore the instruments of the orchestra at the Musical Buffet. Show off in the talent show. Dance, write songs, and make musical instruments. The whole library will be jivin', rockin', and swingin'. Many musical styles will be explored.

Decorate your facility with posters of famous rock stars, jazz musicians, and country singers. Or, use the band ensemble poster provided on p. 81. Do you have some old LP or 45 records at home? Why not hang them from the ceiling? Reading incentives could be kazoos or other inexpensive instruments. A local radio station might give you bumper stickers or other promotional items for reading incentives, too. They might even be willing to do a broadcast from your facility for your end-of-theme party. If your local high school has a jazz band, you may invite them to play a promotional concert at your facility before the school year is over.

Children select their reading from a variety of musical styles from a menu such as the one included on p. 80. Display lots of books in the library with musical themes. Select one hour a week to have music playing in the library, and try to explore many kinds of music including musicals, classical music, blues, hip-hop, and swing. Books and All That Jazz will have readers really humming!

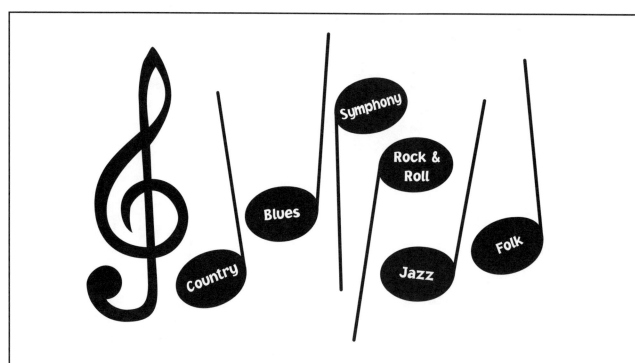

Books and All That Jazz Reading Record

Choose your reading goals from this list.
There are many kinds of music, and many things to read.
Try something new! It will be fun.

1. Country Music. Read three picture books or one chapter book about farms, animals, or country living.

2. Blues. Don't be sad. Read! Read 100 pages or three picture books with a color in the title.

3. Symphony. Since a symphony has three movements that have different moods, choose three picture books or three poems that are different, and then draw a picture including something from each of the three.

4. Jazz. Many jazz songs have interesting rhymes. Read a rhyming picture book or three rhyming poems.

5. Rock & Roll. Rock & roll music has a strong 4/4 beat. Read four picture books, four recipes, four maps, four cereal boxes, four comic strips, four magazines, or four anything!

6. National Folk. Read three picture books, each about a different country. Then, listen to a recording of Latin, Celtic, Asian, African or American folk music.

My Reading Goals: _____

_____

_____

_____

Name: _____

Age: _____

School: _____

Graphics for "Books and All That Jazz" poster

Musical Buffet

A food buffet offers many delicious choices. This *musical* buffet offers many instrumental choices. Children are encouraged to try them all. This program introduces children to the kinds of musical instruments they could choose to play in the school orchestra or band. They will be allowed to hold and try them out. Children will be excited to learn to play their favorite instrument.

Description of Program

Give each child a nametag (see patterns on p. 83). Borrow or rent musical instruments from a music store. First, read a story that involves musical instruments. Then, have someone show children how to hold them and play notes. The program helps children explore a variety of instruments, allowing them to make a better choice when they are ready to learn to play an instrument in school.

Set up a station for each musical family: string instruments, woodwinds, percussion, and brass. Ask people from the music store, from your staff, or from the community to come in and demonstrate how to play the instruments. Try to have one or two instruments from each musical family.

For ages: All

Limit: Any number of children may participate

Length: 1 hour

Staff and volunteer requirements: One adult and four or more volunteers

Volunteer assignments: Volunteers show children how to hold the instrument and how to make a sound with it. The instruction will be very brief for each child, so every child may have a chance to try.

Preparation time: 1–2 hours

Preparation: Call a music store, and arrange to borrow or rent the instruments. Arrange for qualified musicians to demonstrate the instruments. Select a story to read.

Community resources needed: Instruments and instructors for each musical family

Read More About It

Blackwood, Ann. *The Orchestra: An Introduction to the World of Classical Music.* Millbrook Press, 1993. Traces the history of the orchestra, and discusses the musical instruments in the various orchestral families.

Brett, Jan. *Berlioz the Bear.* Putnam, 1991. Berlioz the Bear and his fellow musicians are due to play for the town hall when the mule pulling their bandwagon refuses to move.

Hayes, Ann. *Meet the Orchestra.* Harcourt Brace, 1991. Describes the features, sounds, and role of each musical instrument in the orchestra.

Pinkwater, Daniel. *Bongo Larry.* Marshall Cavendish, 1998. Larry the polar bear's new interest in playing the bongos leads to an impromptu performance with at the Café Mama Bear.

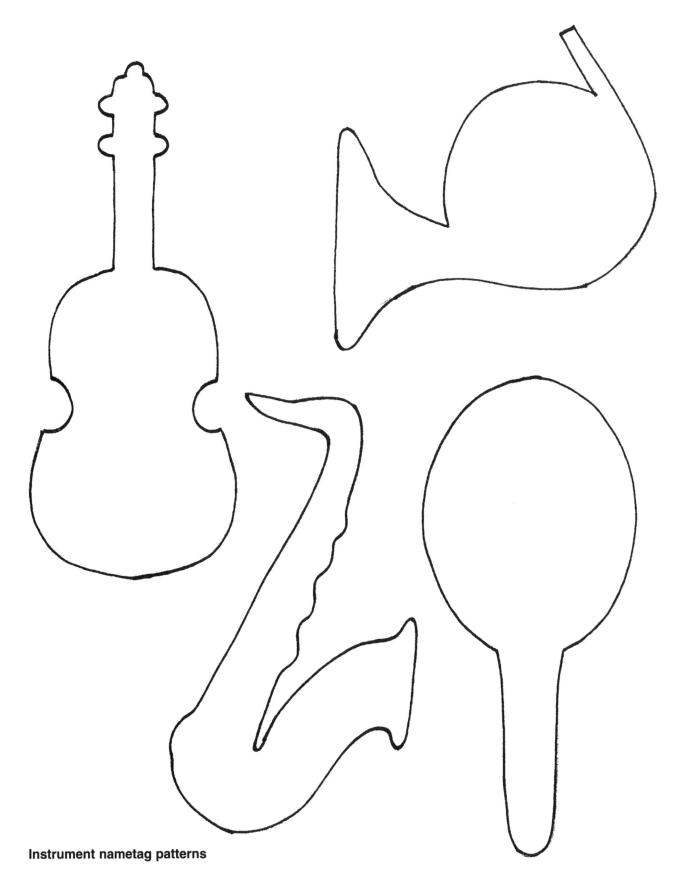

Instrument nametag patterns

Curtains Up! Talent Show

Children are invited to audition for a place on the talent show. The one hour show includes up to 15 acts including dance, instrumental music, vocal music, magic tricks, jumping rope to music, or other performing arts.

Description of Program

One month before the scheduled Talent Show, have volunteer judges audition and select the acts for the show. A suggested maximum of 15 acts of approximately three minutes in length should be selected. It may be possible to use every act in the show. Have an emcee introduce each act on the night of the show with humor or stories to fill in while the next act sets up. If the show includes only a few acts, the emcee may read a story or two at the beginning of the program. At the end of the performance, give each participant a certificate to thank them for sharing their talent. (See sample below.)

For ages: All

Limit: Up to 15 acts may perform, any number may attend the show

Staff and volunteer requirements: One adult and one or two volunteers (or more for crowd control)

Volunteer assignments: Assist with the selection of acts at the auditions. Keep the acts in order off stage, so the show runs with few delays.

Preparation time: 2 hours

Preparation: Announce the auditions. Hold auditions and select the acts. Arrange for an emcee for the show.

Community resources needed: An emcee for the show, which may be a radio personality, the mayor of the town, the school principal, the library director, etc.

Read More About It

Kingland, Robin. *Bus Stop Bop*. Viking, 1991. When the bus breaks down, passengers make the time for repairs pass more quickly by entertaining themselves with an impromptu talent show.

Marshall, James. *Fox on Stage*. Dial Books for Young Readers, 1993. Fox makes a film for Grannie, takes part in a magic show, and puts on a play.

Scott, Ann Herbert. *Brave As A Mountain Lion*. Clarion Books, 1996. Spider is afraid to get up on stage for the school spelling bee.

Tryon, Leslie. *Albert's Play*. Atheneum, 1992. Includes full text of the play "The Owl and the Pussycat." Albert helps the animal children of Pleasant Valley School stage a play.

Curtain's Up Talent Show
Award Certificate

_____
name

Participated in the talent show

_____   _____
Date   Librarian

Sample award certificate

Rock 'n Roll Sock Hop

A family sock hop is a great opportunity for parents and children to enjoy music and dancing together. This program is a fun, intergenerational activity.

Description of Program

Plan a sock hop featuring a variety of classic Rock 'n Roll songs which have been selected for family enjoyment. The music should include funny songs, fast songs, and well-known songs from a variety of decades. If the weather is good, the dance can be held outdoors, and the dance floor can be the parking lot. If the weather is questionable, a large meeting room may be required. A hired DJ supplies a good sound system and speakers, but if you have a volunteer DJ, you may need to arrange for a stereo. Decorate with streamers and sock hop designs. Include a book table with appropriate titles displayed. Use the patterns below to create nametags and/or decorations.

For ages: all

Limit: Any number may participate

Length: 60 minutes

Staff and volunteer requirements: One adult

Preparation time: 1 hour

Preparation: Arrange for the DJ, the stereo, and the location for the dance. Select titles to display on the book table. Publicize the event.

Community resources needed: A professional or volunteer DJ

Read More About It

Classic Rock Digest: *25 Years of Rock 'n' Roll. Compiled by the editors of Goldmine Magazine.* Krause Publications, 1998. Contains biographies and history of the rock and roll legends from 1974 to 1999.

Jackson, John A. *American Bandstand: Dick Clark and the Making of a Rock 'n Roll Empire.* Oxford University Press, 1997. Includes color photos of famous bands and historical and biographical information about rock 'n roll music.

Shirley, David. *The History of Rock & Roll.* Franklin Watts, 1997. Traces the history of rock 'n roll music from the 1950s to the present, and discusses the changing styles and leading personalities.

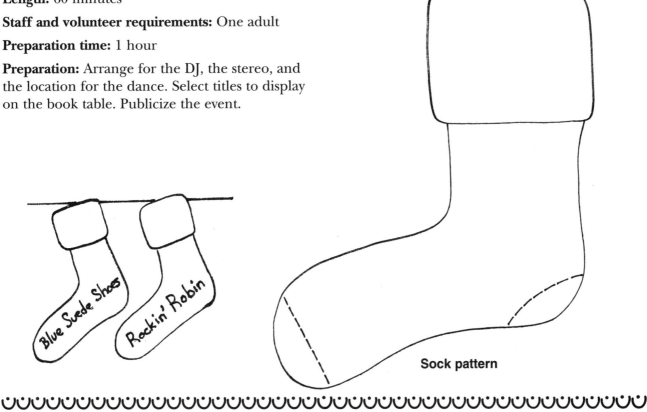

Sock pattern

Hey, Isn't That Elvis?

Children are invited to come to this program dressed as famous musicians and be prepared to tell something about their character.

Description of Program

Decorate the story area with musical notes cut from black posterboard. Have the children dress in costume and introduce their character, telling a little about him or her, including the name of one famous song, or where the person is from. Read a story or stories about famous musicians.

For ages: 5 and up

Limit: Any number of children may participate

Length: 45 minutes

Staff and volunteer requirements: One adult, an optional volunteer

Volunteer assignments: Instruct the children in clapping a leading the beat

Preparation time: 1–2 hours

Preparation: Select music from recordings to play. Arrange for a stereo in the room. Ask a volunteer to teach clapping and leading the music, if needed. Select a story to read.

Activity: Keep the Beat

Many popular songs have a 4/4 beat. Teach children how to clap the beat to a 4/4 song, and how to lead a 4/4 song. Play recordings of a few songs, and help the children clap or lead the beat. Selected music can be from famous musicians, such as: The Beatles, Patsy Cline, Richie Valenz, Mel Torme, Ray Charles, Lois Armstrong, and Elvis Presley.

Did You Know?

Elvis Presley won a local singing contest at age eight, which was his first step toward a musical career.

Louis Armstrong was known by many nicknames, including "Pops," Dippermouth," Satchmo," and "Satch."

Whitney Houston has had more consecutive #1 hits than Elvis Presley or The Beatles.

Patsy Cline's first given name is Virginia. Her first #1 hit was "I Fall to Pieces."

Read More About It

Bego, Mark. *I Fall to Pieces: The Music and the Life of Patsy Cline*. Adams Publications, 1995. A biography with pictures of the famous country singer Patsy Cline.

Benson, Harry. *The Beatles: Now and Then*. Universe Press, 1998. A pictorial history of the Beatles.

Brown, Sanford. *Louis Armstrong*. Franklin Watts, 1993. Examines the personal life and musical career of the famous jazz trumpeter and singer known as "Satchmo."

Frankl, Ron. *Charlie Parker, Musician*. Chelsea House, 1993. Introduces the life and times of noted jazz musician Charlie Parker.

Stanley, David. *The Elvis Encyclopedia*. General Publications Group, 1994. This is a complete reference book on the King of Rock and Roll.

Mardi Gras

The Mardi Gras celebrations in New Orleans always have great jazz music. In this program, the children will make a Mardi Gras mask and enjoy a Cajun snack. They will parade around the story room while listening to jazz music.

Description of Program

Give children craft supplies for decorating a Mardi Gras mask (see p. 88 for pattern). While they are working, read to them or tell them about the Mardi Gras celebration. Serve a Cajun snack as a further introduction to the culture of New Orleans. At the conclusion of the program, have children parade around the story room while jazz music is playing. A good selection for this activity is music from a jazz band, such as "When the Saints Go Marching In."

Some facts to share about Mardi Gras:

- Mardi Gras started long ago as a celebration around mid-February in Ancient Rome.

- Mardi Gras is a celebration to welcome spring and begin Lent. Lent is a season of prayer and fasting observed by the Roman Catholic Church and other Christian churches during the 40 days before Easter Sunday.

- The name, "Mardi Gras" means, "Fat Tuesday" in French. The day is known as Fat Tuesday, because it is the last day before Lenten fasting.

- Rich foods, parades, music, and parties are part of the Mardi Gras celebration.

- The city of New Orleans is famous for their Mardi Gras celebrations.

For ages: 5 and up

Limit: 30 children

Length: 45 minutes

Staff and volunteer requirements: One adult, one optional volunteer

Volunteer assignments: Cut out masks, one for each child. Assist the children with the project.

Preparation time: 2 hours

Preparation: Cut out a mask for each child.

Purchase decorations for the masks. Select a song to play for the parade, and arrange for a stereo in the room. Prepare or purchase a Cajun snack to serve. Select a story to read (*optional*).

Craft: Mardi Gras Mask

Supplies Needed: One mask per child cut from black poster board (pattern on next page), sequins, feathers, beads, tacky glue, elastic chord

The children decorate their Mardi Gras mask by gluing sequins and feathers around the outside edge and on the front. Mardi Gras masks are typically very showy, so plenty of sequins and other decorations can be applied. Attach elastic chord, so the mask may be worn over the face.

Snacks

Snacks for Mardi Gras may include: pralines, cold shrimp with cocktail sauce, red beans and rice, spicy sliced sausage, and hush puppies. Recipes for hush puppies and pralines follow:

Hush Puppies Recipe

¼ c. flour	1 t. black pepper
¾ c. corn meal	1 egg
1 t. salt	¼ c. chopped green onions
2 T. sugar	½ cup buttermilk
1 t. baking powder	1 tablespoon water
¼ t. baking soda	

Combine the dry ingredients. Stir in egg, onion, buttermilk and water. Drop by teaspoons into hot oil. Fry until golden brown.

Pralines Recipe

½ lb. brown sugar	1½ t. butter
pinch of salt	1 c. chopped pecans
¼ c. plus 2 T. evaporated milk	

Mix sugar, salt, milk, and butter in a saucepan. Cook over low heat, stirring constantly with a wooden spoon until sugar dissolves. Stir in pecans, and cook to the soft ball stage, or test with a candy thermometer. The temperature should be 240 degrees Fahrenheit. Remove from heat and stir rapidly until the mixture thickens. Drop by teaspoons 1" apart on waxed paper-lined baking sheets. Let cool until firm.

Read More About It

Coil, Suzanne. *Mardi Gras!* Macmillan Publications, 1994. Examines the history and events connected with the Mardi Gras celebration in New Orleans such as the parades, balls, and "Couris de Mardi Gras."

Prelutsky, Jack. *Beneath A Blue Umbrella: Rhymes.* Greenwillow Books, 1990. A collection of short humorous poems, including one in which children frolic in a Mardi Gras parade.

Shaik, Fatima. *On Mardi Gras Day.* Dial Books for Young Readers, 1999. Two children participating in the traditional Mardi Gras celebration see such sights as the Zulu and Rex parades, enjoying the songs, bright costumes, and gigantic floats.

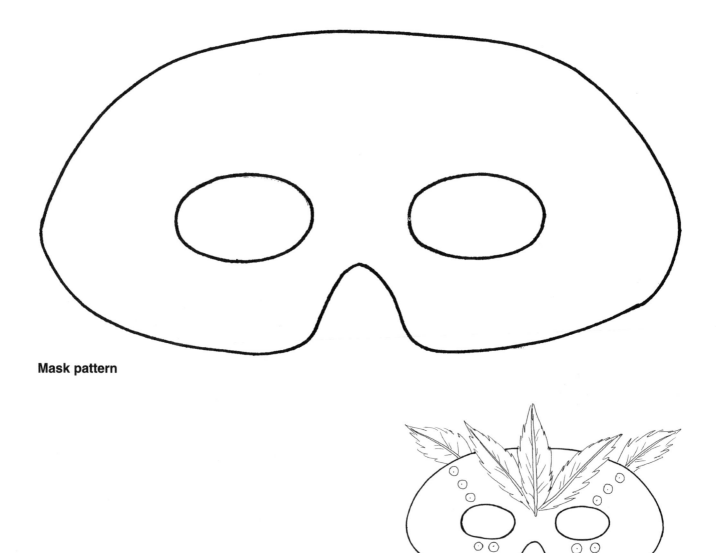

Mask pattern

Sample mask

Make a Musical Instrument

Children enjoy making music with their own bodies, with their voices, and with found objects made into instruments. This program will explore how music is made.

Description of Program

Lead the children in a clapping rhyme and a song. Then discuss with the group how music can be made with our hands and voices. Fill eight glass jars with varying levels of water, and tap on the jars with a spoon, showing the different pitches. Plays a simple song on the jars, such as, "Mary Had A Little Lamb," or "Twinkle, Twinkle, Little Star." Give each child a homemade drum and two craft sticks, and direct the children in a rhythm activity by tapping a rhythm first, then letting them try to play the same rhythm. Give each child a plastic comb and a small piece of waxed paper, and shows the children how to create a kazoo sound by humming through the waxed paper and the comb. The children then form a band with their drums or their kazoos and parade around the room. The "Instruments of the Orchestra" puzzle sheet on p. 90 can be handed out to take home.

For ages: 5 and up

Limit: 30 children

Length: 30 minutes

Staff and volunteer requirements: One adult, one volunteer

Volunteer assignments: Make the drums, cut waxed paper to fit the combs, help with the parade during the program.

Preparation time: 1 hour

Preparation: Assemble the jars and fill with water, then test them and tune them. Prepare to play a song on the jars. (Or arrange for a volunteer to do this.) Prepare to play rhythms on the drums, and hum a tune in the kazoos.

Craft: Musical Instruments

Drums

Supplies Needed: 30 margarine tubs; 30 balloons; 30 rubber bands; 60 craft sticks

Directions: Cut the bottom from each margarine tub with a craft knife. Blow up each balloon without popping it, then let the air out. This will stretch the balloons. Cut open balloons with scissors. Stretch one balloon across the top of each margarine tub and secure with a rubber band. Use two craft sticks for drum sticks.

Water Jar Instrument

Supplies Needed: 8 jelly jars; water; spoon

Directions: Fill one jar nearly full with water. Fill each succeeding jar a little less full. Tap them with a spoon. Tune them by adding or taking out a little water. With a little practice, you may play a simple tune on the instrument. Try "Mary Had A Little Lamb," or "Twinkle, Twinkle, Little Star."

Comb Kazoo

Supplies Needed: Small plastic combs; waxed paper

Directions: Cut waxed paper to the approximate size and shape of the comb. Place the waxed paper and the comb against the lips. Hum a tune. You should hear a buzzing sound as your voice vibrates the paper and the comb.

Read More About It

Parker, Josephine. *Beating the Drum.* Millbrook Press, 1992. Traces the development of drums through various cultures. Includes instructions for making different types of drums.

Sabbeth, Alex. *Rubber Band Banjos and Java Jive Bass: Projects and Activities on the Science of Music and Sound.* John Wiley Press, 1997. Presents the science of sound and music, including how sound is made, how the ear hears sounds, and how different musical instruments are made.

Staples, Danny. *Flutes, Reeds and Trumpets.* Millbrook Press, 1992. Explains how wind instruments work and traces their development through various cultures. Includes directions for making some instruments.

Instruments of the Orchestra

The conductor dropped the score, and all the names of the instruments got scrambled. Can you help him unscramble them?

oobe _____

ritlacen _____

noiap _____

moobrent _____

inaptim _____

lecol _____

vliino _____

nrasdemre _____

tuelf _____

aolvi _____

sssgrinbat _____

pertmut _____

chhnernorf _____

violin

viola

cello

string bass

flute

clarinet

oboe

trumpet

trombone

french horn

timpani

snare drum

piano

Cool Tunes

A Song Writing Workshop

Children create several songs together that they write themselves, using new words for familiar tunes.

Description of Program

Decorate your area with musical notes (see pattern on p. 92). Show the children how to use a familiar tune to create a new song.

For ages: 5 and up

Limit: Any number of children may participate

Length: 30–45 minutes

Staff and volunteer requirements: One adult

Preparation time: 1 hour

Preparation: Practice the songs that will serve as examples for the children.

Activity: Song Writing Workshop

Sing the following songs to the tune of "The Muffin Man," then have the children sing along.

The Violin
I like to play the violin,
the violin, the violin.
I like to play the violin
because it sounds so cool."

The Night Wind
Oh, can you hear the wind at night,
the wind at night, the wind at night.
Oh, can you hear the wind at night.
It sounds alone and sad."

The leader then helps the children create one or more songs of their own for this melody.

Next, the leader sings the following songs to the tune of the "Happy Birthday Song." Explain that the rhyme scheme is AABA, meaning the first, second and last lines rhyme.

Johnny
Johnny's eyes are so blue
And he has freckles, too.
If you asked me if I like him
I would say "Yes, it's true."

Chocolate Ice Cream
I like chocolate ice cream
And hot pies when they steam
I like cup cakes with frosting
And eclairs with whipped cream.

Next, the group tries to create one or more songs with this rhyme scheme and this tune. First, think of three words that rhyme, then try to create the whole song. Some rhymes to try: flower, hour, power; rain, plain, train; sun, fun, one; spring, fling, bring; days, rays, stays.

Finally, try a song that does not rhyme, sung to the "Happy Birthday Song":

I Can
I can run pretty fast.
I can climb a tall tree.
I can use a computer,
I'm a good listener, too.

This kind of song is created out of a list. There is no need to try to rhyme the lines. Now, the group can try to create one or more songs like this.

Read More About It

Blume, Jason. *Six Steps to Songwriting Success: The Comprehensive Guide to Writing and Marketing Hit Songs.* Billboard Books, 1999. Song writing techniques are explored for the serious beginner and the professional song writer.

Dunning, Stephen. *Getting the Knack: 20 poetry Writing Exercises.* National Council of Teachers of English, 1992. Introduces different kinds of poems and provides exercises in writing poems based on memory and imagination.

Livingston, Myra Cohn. *Poem-making: Ways to Begin Writing Poetry.* HarperCollins, 1991. Provides an opportunity for the reader to experience the joy of making a poem.

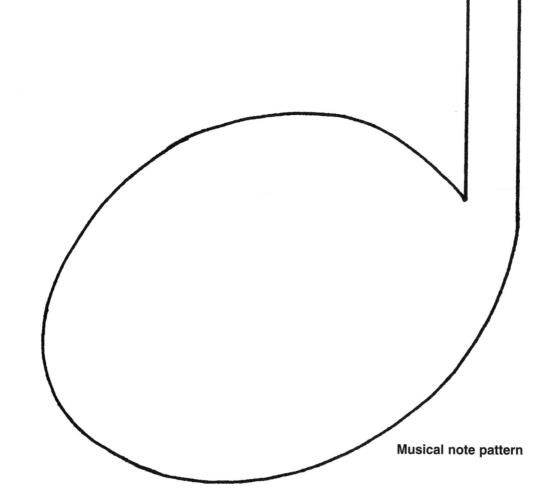

Musical note pattern

Caroling in July Service Project

Everyone loves to sing familiar songs, and it's even more fun to make up new words to old tunes. This program features a number of carols-turned-reading songs.

Description of the Program

This service project requires parents and children to learn some new words to familiar Christmas carols. The group sings for an audience at a location of your choice in the community. Some places to consider are nursing homes, hospitals, or malls.

Select a leader for the singing, and arrange for someone to play a portable keyboard or guitar accompaniment. Caroling is usually quite casual, so there is no need to get too concerned about making the performance professional quality.

Let people know about your service project in late May or early June. Arrange for several practice times. A good time for practice would be just before or just after the regular story time, when people are already at the library. On the day of your performance, families should meet at the library. Practice the songs again for 15 minutes, then caravan to the place where you will be singing. After the performance you may want to gather for popcorn and punch at the library or a park.

For ages: All

Limit: Any number may participate

Staff and volunteer requirements: One adult, one volunteer

Volunteer assignment: Lead the practices and the performance of the singing.

Preparation time: 2 hours

Preparation: Find a volunteer to lead the singing. Arrange for a place for the performance. Purchase snacks for the celebration after the performance. Make copies of the words to the songs for all of the singers. Publicize the project and the concert.

Caroling in July: Songs About Reading

Gather 'Round
(to the tune of "Deck the Halls")
Gather 'round. We'll read a story.
Fa la la la la la la la la
Knights and Kings in all their glory.
Fa la la la la la la la la
Read a page or read a chapter
Fa la la la la la la la la
We'll live happily ever after
Fa la la la la la la la la

Happy Summer
(to the tune of "We Wish You A Merry Christmas")
We wish you a happy summer,
we wish you a happy summer,
we wish you a happy summer
with good books to read.

Well, summer's the time
to read and to play.
So have fun together
and read every day.

We wish you a happy summer, we wish you a happy summer, we wish you a happy summer with good books to read."

Jolly Old Librarian
(to the tune of "Jolly Old St. Nicholas")
Jolly old librarian,
lean your ear this way.
Don't you tell a single soul
what I'm going to say.

Summer time is coming soon.
Tell you what I need.

A really, really, really, really,
real good book to read.

Johnny wants a fantasy,
Kristen wants adventures.
Grandpa wants a real thick book.
That's where he puts his dentures.

As for me, librarian,
I'm not hard to please.
I just want a really, really,
real good book to read.

Great Summer
(to the tune of "White Christmas")

I'm dreaming of a great summer,
just like the ones I used to know.
With treetops swaying and children playing
and singing by the campfire's glow.

I'm dreaming of a great summer
with a good book to read at night.
May each book you read be a delight,
and may every ending be just right.

The Library
(to the tune of "Little Drummer Boy")

Come, they told me, to the library.
You'll have a real good time at the library.
CDs and videos at the library.
They have the Internet at the library,
the library, the library.
Lots of books to read at the library.
The library.

A Book to Read
(to the tune of "All I Want for Christmas")

All I want this summer is a book to read,
a book to read, a book to read.

All I want this summer is a book to read.
Then I will say, "Happy summer!"

Read A Book
(to the tune of "Let It Snow")

Oh, the weather outside is sunny.
And you don't have lots of money.
But you want something fun to do...
Read a book, read a book, read a book.

After playing outside awhile,
I asked Mom "What can I do?"
Then she said with a happy smile,
"I'll read a book with you."

Now the sunset is softly glowing,
and the breeze is gently blowing.
Let's find a spot just for two,
and Read a book, read a book, read a book."

Read More About It

Guback, Georgia. *The Carolers.* Greenwillow, 1992. A group of carolers go from house to house as they share the beauty of Christmas with others. Lyrics to the carols they are singing are included.

Hopkinson, Deborah. *A Band of Angels: A Story Inspired by the Jubilee Singers.* Atheneum, 1999. The daughter of a slave forms a gospel singing group and goes on tour to raise money to save Fisk University.

Peterson, Jeanne Whitehouse. *My Mama Sings.* HarperCollins, 1994. Mama sings all the time, but one day when she is feeling blue and has no song to sing, her little boy makes up a song for her.